SUITED MONK LEADERSHIP

*Leading with Wisdom and Purpose in a
Complex and Uncertain World*

Raf Adams and Mike Thompson

WOW Books

First published in June 2014 by WOW Books, a division of The Good Brand Works Ltd., Impact Hub Kings Cross, 34B York Way, London N1 9AB.

Fine tuning editorial work was completed by the Script Doctor, Mark Stibbe. Typesetting by Paul Minett.

ISBN 978-0-9570553-7-7

WOW Books
Impact Hub Kings Cross
34B York Way
London N1 9AB

www.suitedmonk.com

CONTENTS

FOREWORD

by Peter Buytaert, Chief Responsibility Officer, Good Leaders Online

Over the past 25 years, I have experienced the joy of collaboration with leaders who are true to themselves and embrace a greater purpose in life. They know the pain and struggle of dealing with those who are unable to align outer world success with true happiness and this experience usually results in the destructive power of office politics, stress and potential burnout.

Eight years ago, as a next step in my personal journey to self-realisation (described in chapter 2), I realised both the truth and the power of what we now call Suit and Monk alignment when I decided to trust the energy of my heart and take a leap of faith. I have ever since built and led teams around one key premise:

How can I help people self-realise, help them to find passion and purpose in their work and build a good company in the process?

Trusting your gut and finding true happiness and purpose in life and career are extremely powerful motivators for both executives and the organisations that engage them. The more self-aware we become, the more we will display humility and respect. We will develop the quality of our leadership and utilise resources to achieve personal and company success, attracting even better leadership in the process.

Especially in our world of high volatility, uncertainty, complexity and ambiguity (VUCA), the self-awareness, humane character and intuitive insights of leadership are increasingly and rightfully validated in both academic and business literature as key competencies to wisely navigate the new frontiers of the 21st Century.

Dr. Mike Thompson and Raf Adams are both good friends and colleagues who have inspired me with their arguably prophetic insight into this power of wisdom in leadership and the degree to which it can make the world a more harmonious place. This book is timely in a world that is undergoing a paradigm shift and which needs responsible leaders to stand up and bring us to the place where companies put purpose alongside profit and where values are honoured over greed, while showing humility and respect across global cultures. Moving away from a focus on rational (IQ) capability, the authors encourage us to use intuitive power, humane character and emotional stability as critical leadership attributes for the 21st Century.

The experience, passion and spiritual insights of Raf, with his ground-level exposure to China as the arriving new superpower, combined with Mike's research and academic exposure on a global level, form a powerful synergy designed to enlighten us about how the Suited Monk Leader will make a difference for us and our organisations at large.

I can validate that their insights have been and will be very much a part of my own journey in progressing my leadership. Whether you are a corporate executive or a startup entrepreneur, the better you know and express your true self, the more intuitive power you will awaken and the easier it will become to catch the flow of life and find your path to purpose and happiness in the process. It requires courage though to make that happen and this book will support you on that path.

In my organisation, we always invite our people to find their 'Monk' and align their values and life journey with the company. It is the best motivator and retention strategy when people feel empowered to realise their own happiness while contributing to the good purpose of the company. We obviously pursue profit, but not at the expense of values and purpose.

I invite you to join me in reading *Suited Monk Leadership* and become an advocate of the new type of leadership that this world so urgently requires.

Peter Buytaert,
Shanghai,
April 2014

Raf and Mike express their grateful appreciation for the wise editorial assistance given by Peter Buytaert in the writing of Suited Monk Leadership.

INTRODUCTION

Volatility, Uncertainty, Complexity and Ambiguity (VUCA) are new challenges that face us all in an increasingly interdependent world which demands a new type of leadership with higher intuitive power and humane character to complement rational (IQ) capabilities.

More and more we realise and experience our interdependency on one another in the new multi polar world where globalisation and localised needs often conflict yet require co-existence. The Knowledge Economy has given way to the 'Big Data'* Economy but also to an economy that has been forced to address social justice and sustainable living. Some business leaders call this 'Conscious Capitalism' in which good purpose and profits become equally important pillars to build business. Some

---

* Big Data is a collection of data sets so large and complex that it becomes difficult to process.

of this is coming about as a result of new law, international standards and reporting frameworks, and investor pressure. But it is also possible that a greater sense of what is humane in the midst of a VUCA world is another driver behind more and more businesses re-thinking their true purpose for long term sustainability. We believe that all these trends are giving rise to a new breed of leadership driven with purpose and a vision for the Common Good to balance short term business requirements.

What are key challenges facing this new leadership in the VUCA world?

The VUCA world is **volatile** with rapid and unpredictable change. The VUCA world is now the norm of our everyday experience. Managers face new kinds of problems making the fixed 'five year' business plan obsolete in an exponentially changing environment. We have witnessed volatility in financial markets whereby local events in one market caused a tsunami in world markets – the 'bad' home loan mortgages in the US in 2007-08 is one notable example. The rate of change in the way businesses operate is occurring faster than ever, fuelled by globalisationand technological breakthroughs.

Uncertainty surrounds us despite the apparent assurance of ever more Big Data. We do not know what is going to happen one week from now in our business life (sometimes our personal lives too). As Bank of England economist, Andy Haldane, has pointed out: 'Fully defining future states of the world, and probability-weighting them, is beyond anyone's cognitive limits.'[1] Despite more information, we seem to be less certain about financial markets, world economic and political developments. Health scares, climate change scenarios, scarcity of resources, economic modelling that few trust, and the now normal uncertainty over how we make provision for our financial security, including retirement plans, affect us on a personal level.

The VUCA world is also filled with **complexity**. This is because we are more interdependent than ever for our survival. This in turn greatly intensifies the complex connections that we establish in order to express this interdependence. Social media networks, virtual communities and 'real time' news present opportunities and challenges to comprehend and master.

Complexity science has gathered scientists from across disciplines to find common principles underlying the behaviour of complex systems—systems in which large collections of components interact in nonlinear ways. Who can comprehend all possible data available to make an informed decision? Melanie Mitchell, Professor of Computer Science at Portland State University, is amongst the complex systems scientists trying to help us find ways of understanding complexity: 'In our era of Big Data, what Complexity potentially offers is "Big Theory" - a scientific understanding of the complex processes that produce the data we are drowning in.'[2] Whatever help science provides, each business leader has to cope emotionally and psychologically with the heightened complexity of the commercial world.

Ambiguity arises at least in part from the fact that our words and actions can be interpreted differently amongst colleagues across cultures, political sensitivities and diverse stakeholder groups. Religious diversity and cross cultural differences force leaders to look at the same challenges through different glasses applying the belief systems that surround them. A foreign executive in China may not immediately grasp why building relationships *(guanxi)* is a vital part for success unless he or she understands the place of *guanxi* in social and business relationships.

In light of the speed of change, leaders are under pressure to make decisions faster while struggling with increased complexity, ambiguity and unpredictability. Relying only on rational analysis will not lead to the highest quality of decision-making which requires a broad range of inputs, both rational and non-rational. Now, more than ever, leaders need to learn to apply their intuitive power to distil the right decisions.

In a knowledge economy, leaders can rely on data collection and rational processes. In a VUCA world this worldview needs to be supplemented with intuitive thinking and humane character.

Humane character requires a high degree of self-awareness and authenticity. As human beings we are amazingly unique and complex. We can show incredible weakness and frailty but also extraordinary strength and ingenuity. Following many conversations with business leaders and middle managers, some more formally by survey, we have found that the common thread is a desire for more leadership authenticity.

In a VUCA world, people follow leaders of integrity. These are men and women who succeed because they give hope, courage and a vision for the good of society built on integrity. In essence, they are wise leaders.

As a sequel to Raf's book, *The Suited Monk: Finding Your Life's Purpose And True Happiness*, *Suited Monk Leadership* delves more deeply into wise leadership practice by helping the reader to understand their personal and professional lives in the forms of their Suit and Monk and how they can best align these two parts to achieve more authentic leadership.

The Suited Monk started with an original idea to think about how we can develop a life and career that includes both our internal spiritual journey (our Monk) with our life in the external world (our Suit) so that we can be happy and fulfilled on the inside and achieve success in the world of our Suit and career. Our Suit represents our social identity: our role at work, with friends and in relation to our community or nation. We wear a suit for business meetings, a suit for social occasions and a suit for special events. The Suit is a metaphor for the way we project ourselves into the external world and is adjusted for different social environments. For example, your job title is part of your Suit. Our Monk is our inner world of passions, motivations, values and purpose that brings us true happiness.

In *The Suited Monk*, Raf takes the reader on a journey of self-awareness and how to identify and bridge the Gap between your Suit and your Monk. In *Suited Monk Leadership*, we complement this personal awareness journey by outlining and illustrating the behaviours and characteristics demanded of leadership in the 21st VUCA century.

The topics that we shall cover are designed to help Suited Monk Leaders to:

- Develop humane character with higher self-awareness and authenticity
- Close the Gap between their Suit and Monk
- Cultivate intuitive thinking in decision making
- Trust the Flow in life
- Enhance company values with 'virtuous' leadership, and the long term value of ethical and wise decision-making
- Communicate effectively by applying Suit-Monk strategies to touch the hearts of people they lead
- Align their teams with hope, courage and a vision that incorporates a purpose that contributes to the Common Good of society
- Ultimately align rational thinking with humane character, intuitive power on a basis of emotional stability: in essence to lead wisely.

Signs of Suited Monk Leadership in Business

Suited Monk Leaders are already active in large and small companies. The business leaders known as the 'B Team,' who see the purpose of business as 'a driving force for social, environmental and economic benefit,'[3] are examples of people who have connected their business expertise with a passion to make a positive difference in the world.

Management guru, Peter Drucker, questioned whether knowledge-based leadership alone would be sufficient for the moral challenges that he envisaged would emerge from the knowledge economy produced by late twentieth century capitalism.[3] The political and economic turmoil of recent years has taught us about the moral limitations of the knowledge economy. We need more than knowledge to combat the desire for power and money through the exploitation of human and natural resources. Businesses need a capacity for decision-making which can weigh potential impacts on society and the environment beyond the immediate demands of the market or scientific advancement. Drucker is clear that such decisions will be made 'neither on "scientific" nor on "factual" grounds. It must be a choice between values and based on highly subjective appraisals of the future.' He was hinting at an approach beyond the rational domain and this book is one attempt to plot out a course that complements a rational approach to leadership with another way of leading and living.

In *Suited Monk Leadership* we aim to show how you can tap into your real self to live and lead with purpose, insight and self-awareness to enjoy the good life with strong interpersonal skills and wise competencies. Wisdom cannot easily be defined; it's easier to think about people whom we admire for their wisdom. They make judgements which demonstrate real concern for others, not just themselves. In making judgments they integrate their rational capability with intuitive insight (often based on experience) and integrity. They are able to regulate their emotions and have a high sense of self-awareness and empathy. We explain more in chapter 10: 'The Wisdom of a Suited Monk'. We believe that as we participate in an ever interconnected VUCA world so the next stage in human development goes beyond knowledge and towards a wiser form of leadership in our organisations and companies: leadership with wisdom, purpose and vision and towards a form of capitalism and social intelligence that increasingly attempt to integrate profit-making aims with doing good for people and planet.

Many leaders burn out or lose their way because of focusing on their Suit. Corporate scandals are increasingly reported in the public domain and society is losing trust in companies. Less than one in five respondents in the 2013 Edelman Trust Barometer believes a business or governmental leader will actually tell the truth. For business leaders the trust statistics are even worse: trust in business leaders to tell the truth is only 18 percent.[4] As leaders move towards a global mindset, we believe that the momentum is growing to shift motivation in organisations from individual ego gratification towards team collaboration and a vision for the common good.

Over the past several years we have been working in Asia with the Suited Monk concept to develop a global mindset which taps into our own sense of awareness, values and purpose in life and business. Cultivating personal values, integrity and leading with purpose has become a more explicit goal in the emerging generation of leaders. At the year end, when employee development plans and needs are conducted, more employees are searching for a better work-life balance and greater meaning and happiness at work. HR specialists continue to search for solutions to meet the needs of the employee Monk with the business demands on the employee Suit.

Some companies are already taking initiatives to help employees become more self-aware and mindful in their personal and professional lives. DHL China, for example, have an employee development plan called 'Happy Work – Happy Life'. From 2014 the company evolved this plan to become a vital part of their strategy. Companies such as Bayer, Mead Johnson and BASF are now offering personal development programs on self-awareness and 'Leading from Within'.

Suited Monk Leadership offers an alternative approach to develop leaders, to cultivate their wisdom and to develop a greater self-awareness. Most leaders have developed a good Suit: analytical skills, data driven and usually an MBA. But the Monk is often neglected by management education and skills training programmes. This book is aimed to help you to cultivate your Monk and help you to manage the pressures on your Suit.

We hope that our book will be just one aid to help you to navigate a path across the bumpy and complex terrain of life – especially in the context of career and organisational life. Harmonising our Suit with our Monk is, for us, the way to live life well. An enlarged Suit and a squashed Monk cannot bring deep-seated happiness. Although we may find that our Monk has been a little squashed, the good news is that our Monk can be brought alive to guide us through the pressures of the complex world in which we live.

1. Haldane, A., 2012, "The dog and the frisbee". A paper presented to Federal Reserve Bank of Kansas City's 36th economic policy symposium, "The Changing Policy Landscape", Jackson Hole, Wyoming, 31 August.

2. Mitchell, M., 2014, "How Can the Study of Complexity Transform Our Understanding of the World?" www.bigquestionsonline.com/content/how-can-study-complexity-transform-our-understanding-world

3. See: http://bteam.org

4. Drucker, P. F., 1968, *The Age of Discontinuity: Guidelines to Our Changing Society*, *Transaction*, New Brunswick and London., p.372.

5. Edelman, 2013, "2013 Edelman Trust Barometer Finds a Crisis in Leadership". http://www.edelman.com/trust-downloads/press-release/

1. YOUR SUIT AND MONK

A good head and a good heart are always a formidable combination
Nelson Mandela[1]

Why do you get up in the morning and go to work? Why do your employees go to work? What is the purpose of your leadership? Why do you do the things you do? Raf asks these questions in company workshops and finds that the common answer is 'to make a living so we can take care of our family' or, 'I never really reflected on that'. Taking care of family is obviously a very good reason for work, but we rarely hear answers like, 'because I love my job', or, 'because I believe I am contributing to our company purpose in helping people to live a better quality of life,' or, 'I am fulfilled by the work that I do.' For some, the purpose of work is a means to an end but part of a fulfilled and happy life is discovering how we can best use our gifts through work.

As we go through school life, we learn about economics, history, languages, mathematics, sciences and so on - all important subjects to develop our minds, or what we call our Suits. Leaders in organisations build up their Suit through certificated skills courses and often an MBA to enhance their performance and career development. This is an important part of education but it is only one arc in the journey of our lives.

However, there is another arc to our life which is hidden but equally important. When Raf asks people in his workshops what they learned about life's purpose, or how they could develop their unique talents in school, no one raises their hand. Teachers are focused on getting their students through a curriculum of study and it is difficult for them to create space for developing individual gifts and purpose.

The result is that many of us are not sufficiently educated to consider meaning, values and purpose in life, nor are we empowered to develop intuition or an ethical instinct, unless we received that kind of education in our family. The education process is about educating our minds or Suits but does not address our perceptions of the world from within – the real 'me', the Monk beneath the Suit. As a result many of us become lost in the direction of our career; we don't really know what we want.

Frequently we use the word 'heart' to refer to our

true self and the place where our talents, deep beliefs and feelings 'reside'. Sometimes heart is juxtaposed with head when we grapple with conflicting views in making a decision - as in 'head and heart'. Our head, or our mind, includes our personal beliefs, fears and perceptions of reality; it projects the roles we choose or which are given to us by our social context, our external world. Another word used for the way we project ourselves into the external world is ego. The ego has a tendency to drive us to perform which can be good if the drive comes from an inner purpose and is aligned with our talents but can cause stress if there is no heart or Monk engaged.

The Suit is usually developed through learning the rules of the game in a particular social context. The Suit is adept at acquiring the knowledge and skills that we need to be professionally effective – and we need these skills. The Suit is especially focused on tangible and measurable outcomes: targets, KPI's and numbers. Most people focus on the Suit because the outcomes are measurable and give us an idea of how we perform in our job. We may have the tendency to measure life success by career performance but what is the difference between our career performance and how *happy* we are, or our career performance and how *unhappy* we are? This is an important question which is perhaps one reason why in February 2014 J.P.Morgan encouraged their employees to use their employee-assist-ance program to manage stress and depression following three suicides by executives who had all the signs of successful career performance.

Our Suit in the organisational world exercises rational strengths, balances objectivity with personal advantage and is very good at executing plans (although not always successfully). It likes systems, rules, models and processes. The better your Suit performs, the happier your stakeholders, family and level of success seem to be. Suits operate very well when rational thinking is required, such as when analysing data. But the onset of 'Big Data' can also be a source of angst for the Suit simply because of the availability of vast and complex data points for managerial decision-making. We can feel overwhelmed as we try to find the right conclusions from the data. In other words, there comes a point when our rational capacity 'creaks' and we need to be able to view the challenges from another perspective. This perspective is often referred to as the 'gut feel' of intuitive insight. The HR Director of a large fashion retailer shared with us that the boss explicitly exercises decision-making based on 60% data collection after which gut kicks in to make a decision. In the VUCA world, we need to be able to use Big Data with poise, unphased by its complexity, uncertainty and ambiguity. Easier said than done! We hope to show that by living from our Monk, our ability to handle such challenges as Big Data is improved because we respond from a different place of being.

When we refer to heart or spirit or Monk, we are referring to the true potential that lies in each individual.

The true heart of a human being is energy or spirit but because most people can't see it they tend to ignore it and only pay attention to the outside world. The Suit is tangible, the Monk is intangible.

So who is the real you beneath your Suit and what is your true purpose of being here on planet earth? The real you is unique; you are unique in your gifts, competencies, passions, hopes and visions. Your Suit is on display through your daily interactions with people and through your lifestyle and possessions. Your Monk is within and can sometimes be squashed by the activity and stresses of your Suit. Your Monk carries a sense of purpose, perhaps many purposes, but we are often not conscious of this voice within.

One of the challenges facing HR professionals is to find people who have a correct assessment of their strengths and weaknesses. This means high self-awareness and also a sense of humility about abilities and talents. Assessment centres and workshops with various psycho-metric tests provide a reality check on candidates who may have a higher view of their abilities than is the reality.

One example of Suit-work to improve performance is the 'Act As If' approach. The philosopher, William James, believed that it isn't that our feelings guide our actions (feel happy and you will laugh) but rather it is our actions that guide our emotions (laugh and you will feel happy). This means if you want to effect a change in your emotions or behaviour, you should act ' as if' you already have made the change. While there is no question that this technique can effect behavioural change it is focussed on your identity and behaviour in the external world. The internal Gap can remain unchanged because your Suit is doing the work. Behaviour that comes from skill is also temporary.

You always have two resources on your side to help you towards self-mastery: your Suit and your Monk. It is up to you to decide which you would like to call on for help, and when. It can be hard to choose between your Suit and your Monk because both have solutions to offer. For example, when you want to launch a new product, your Suit may help you in analysing markets and deriving strategy to provide tangible information. And your Monk will give you a gut feel to complement this with intangible insights and foresights or a sense of knowing what is the right approach to take. Jenna, a senior sportswear executive assigned to China, explained that despite a well structured market research report being conducted by a Big Five consulting firm, the real market insights were ultimately derived from complementing the data with her gut feel after heading into the streets, the retail stores and by talking to customers. She realised that Big Data needed to be complemented with intuitive insights resulting in invaluable new ways to connect with the Chinese consumer. Without using both Suit and Monk resources, Jenna would probably have arrived at the wrong conclusions potentially costing the company both time and money.

Tasks can be accomplished peacefully, even in the

midst of high pressure, if you can interact with both your Suit and your Monk and get them working together as a team. Generally input and insight from your Monk comes first and then the Suit-work of execution follows.

The Gap

Have you ever 'stretched the truth' in your CV to overplay your credentials? If you have touched up your CV in describing your achievements in previous jobs, or phrased academic references in a way that is not entirely accurate, how do you feel? Have you ever made decisions which are not in line with your true self? Initially you might feel good about bolstering your identity and making yourself more impressive and capable. But deep down within, you know you are not being true to yourself and you can feel it. In those moments a Gap has been created.

Your mind feels good about the decision but your heart feels uncomfortable. Between the heart and the mind there is a feeling of unease; the source of this feeling is what we call the Gap.

We believe that to realise and fulfil your life purpose in the VUCA world, your Suit and Monk have to work in harmony. At birth your Suit and Monk are, as it were, in harmony because you are born 'complete', 'whole' and 'one person.' In other words, your inner and external worlds are not at this stage separated. It is only as a child grows into adulthood that the Suit begins to develop as a sense of social identity is formed. The subsequent socialisation process can often result in a separation between our Suit and our Monk. This separation is the Gap between the life that people are living externally and the life that they really want which is held in their inner world. You can be successful externally but lack meaning and purpose internally.

Think of your Gap as a container of water. Every time you take an action in which you are not true to yourself, or in which you know you are being unethical, water is added to the container. Sometimes you only add two or three drops of water to the container at a time, for instance, by telling little lies. More water is added if you take a bribe or tell stories which don't hold true.

The more 'water' you carry around, the bigger the burden you feel and the more you suffer with anxiety as you struggle to keep up the image and stories you have created. The more stories you tell which are not in line with who you are, the greater the burden you carry and the more pressure you have because you need to make up stories to cover up other stories. All may appear to work out well when no one finds out, but how often can you sustain storytelling, and what is happening to your Monk inside when you do? If people eventually find out that you have lied, the pain is bigger than the gain. Reputational damage to a company is significant when facts are hidden or distorted by a company's leaders.

Sometimes the drive for career success, the promotion of the egoic self, the need and desire to possess things and the search for pleasure result in an exclusive orientation toward things in the external world. When your focus is solely on the external world and in pleasing others for personal gain, you too become increasingly disconnected from your authentic self. The diagram below illustrates the Gap that creates stress and pressure and shows how fears and beliefs can drive our Ego / Suit further away from our Spirit / Monk.

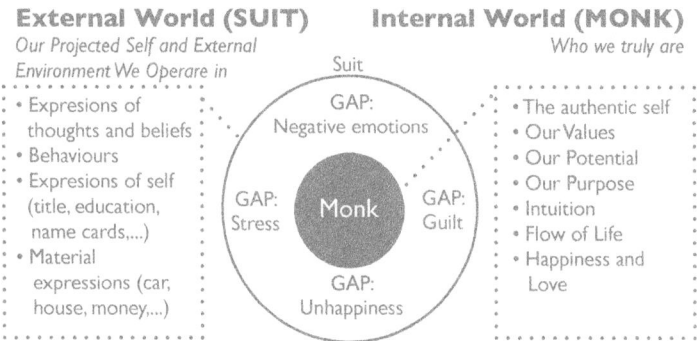

External World (SUIT)

Our Projected Self and External Environment We Operate in

- Expressions of thoughts and beliefs
- Behaviours
- Expressions of self (title, education, name cards,...)
- Material expressions (car, house, money,...)

Suit

GAP: Negative emotions

GAP: Stress

Monk

GAP: Guilt

GAP: Unhappiness

Internal World (MONK)

Who we truly are

- The authentic self
- Our Values
- Our Potential
- Our Purpose
- Intuition
- Flow of Life
- Happiness and Love

GAP EFFECT on Power as an example

Power used without Suit Monk alignment	Power used with Suit Monk alignment
When suit and monk are not aligned power is used to 'cure' gaps in unhappiness and stress, driven by ego and pursuing self gratification. This power often results in non ethical behaviour and lack of integrity.	When suit and monk are aligned and there is no gap, power is used to influence for good purpose. Power is based on ethical value and integrity

The Gap can make leaders less or more effective depending on how they manage themselves. Personal effectiveness as a leader, as well as integrity and optimal self-management, are achieved when the Suit and Monk become more closely aligned and the Gap closes. If the

Suit and Monk are not aligned, the Gap causes people to make unethical and unwise decisions emanating from a lack of self-awareness. These can result in a loss of self-respect and the respect of others.

Big Gaps can be damaging

The regularity of media stories of well-respected leaders in business, politics, sport or entertainment falling in some way from positions of respect and admiration is striking. The need for power and glory can be exacerbated when you are in a high profile position in life. As a result the Gap between the public life and private life of such people is more likely to be exposed. Gap failures can mean the breaking of trust or the exploitation of others through fraud or psychological manipulation. Lance Armstrong had a great Suit; he was arguably one of the greatest cyclists in the world, a man who raised the profile of cycling as a sport. He won the Tour de France seven times and won an Olympic bronze medal. He became famous for his inspiring fight against testicular cancer and the subsequent launch of the Lance Armstrong Foundation to support the needs of those suffering from cancer. Armstrong became a hero to young cyclists around the world. But the admiration was for his Suit and for his celebrity profile and status. He was thought to be 'an all-round good guy.'

But was he really a good guy? He was certainly smart, athletic, philanthropic and media friendly? But was he wise and good in his role as a cyclist's hero? Only a few people knew that there was a big Gap between the real Lance Armstrong and the Suit that seemed to be so admirable. In 2012, he was stripped of seven Tour de France titles and banned for life from competitive cycling. In January 2013 the International Olympic Committee asked Armstrong to return the bronze medal he won at the Olympic Games in Sydney. He resigned from the Foundation that he had established and the Armstrong Foundation was renamed the Livestrong Foundation. After years in which he rebutted accusations of doping, the U.S. Anti-Doping Agency issued a report detailing widespread doping by Armstrong and his teammates. The report called it the 'most sophisticated doping program in sports'. The world's media conveyed stories of disgrace and shame. A sporting hero once admired across the world was regarded in press commentary as a cheat and a bully. At the time, media coverage emphasised Armstrong's apparent lack of remorse. This shows how our Monk not only seeks to see through a Suit but looks for an acknowledgment of wrongdoing. But big Suits try to suppress such acknowledgments. When Suit and Monk are aligned then remorse over mistakes and failings becomes more natural. Expressions of apology and genuine sorrow bring healing not only to the person but to others who have been injured.

To Armstrong's credit, he did express sorrow in his interview with Oprah Winfrey in January 2013. When she asked him if he was a bully, Armstrong, replied, 'Yes,

I was a bully. I was a bully in the sense that I tried to control the narrative and if I didn't like what someone said I turned on them.'[2] He admitted to living a big lie and that he was a 'flawed character'. The consequences of one man's moral failure are impossible to assess when one considers the honest cyclists who were unable to beat Armstrong and others who were using drugs to gain an advantage unfairly.

Lance Armstrong has not told us how he lost his conscience in using drugs to help him win races. Perhaps the power of the Suit had completely overwhelmed the voice of his inner Monk. Once the Gap between Monk and Suit starts to balloon it is very difficult to take back control. Often a crisis, like being stripped of seven Tour de Force medals, hits the Suit so hard that we see our lives in a new way and we take the shaky path to connect to a different Life Journey arc. Perhaps you can recall such a time in your own life. How did you respond then? One way is to 'bury' the Monk and toughen up the Suit to avoid the hurt and pain of a large Gap in your life. Life can actually become quite small then even if you achieve material success. Bitterness can do its worst as the Suit marches forward to pursue its own ends even if it can create the appearance of being concerned for others.

The Smart but Foolish Gap

Many high profile leaders in sport or in business would be admired for being smart. Mike remembers in his early career first hearing the word 'smart' in the descriptions of people and wondered if he was in the 'smart group' as it seemed to be quite an important social reference point for some people. Smart is a buzz word for a person's intelligence, mental speed, and grasp of issues in the world; it is associated with success. These measures are central in today's education system. Children are graded on how smart they are based on logic but only certain schools balance this with educating a child to understand their talents, gifts, purpose and true self. Some children create negative self-beliefs because they don't get the best grades. Classroom ranking creates the perception that being smart is the gateway to success and happiness.

In April 2013, we were conducting a half-day open session in Shanghai at the British Chamber of Commerce for business professionals on helping them to make better decisions in their life and career. At the end of the workshop a Chinese lady called Sharon stood up and asked, 'What is the difference between being smart and being wise when making decisions? Often smart people are seemingly more successful so what should we pursue?' That was a good question and we replied that smart people are not necessarily wise and wise people are not necessarily 'smart' if smartness is defined as being knowledgeable, with a fast mind and a good set of educational certificates. Wise people have insight and a sense of intuition and foresight but are not necessarily smart by IQ measurement.

Let's explore the smart-wise distinction further. Bill George wrote a Harvard Business School Blog in 2011 entitled 'Why Leaders Lose Their Way'. He cited the fall of some well known business leaders and senators, all generally acknowledged as being smart people, high achievers and strong leaders. But they fell due to unethical or criminal activities. George poses the questions we all ask when we observe failings by well-known leaders in business, politics or sport:

Why do leaders known for integrity and leadership engage in unethical activities?
Why do they risk great careers and unblemished reputations for such ephemeral gains?
Do they think they won't get caught or believe their elevated status puts them above the law?[3]

George points out the risks of power at the top: loneliness, paranoia, the tendency of work to take over the whole ofone's life and the danger of losing touch with reality. He notices that fallen leaders 'shut down their inner voice, because it is too painful to confront or even acknowledge'.

'Why Smart People Can Be So Foolish' was the title of an article written in 2004 by Professor Robert Sternberg, a leading wisdom psychologist. He posed the question: 'Can a person be smart, in the sense of knowing all the facts he or she needs to know and then some, and at the same time be foolish in some sense?'[4] In Sternberg's view foolishness is the opposite of wisdom. Many behaviours by smart people are not so much stupid, in the sense of unintelligent, as foolish, in the sense of unwise.

So why do people in power, smart leaders, sometimes act so foolishly? Sternberg's answer is that they often acquire five dispositions that dispose them to foolishness: unrealistic optimism, egocentrism, a sense of omniscience, a sense of omnipotence, and a sense of invulnerability. This is the description of a Suit that has 'gone wrong' – an egocentric Suit. The Suit has become so inflated that it has overwhelmed a person's Monk. This causes the Gap between a person's Suit and Monk to become enormous. One of the casualties of such a Gap is often the destruction of personal relationships and one's true self.

'SORRY, I COULDN'T SEE YOU BEHIND ALL THAT WEALTH AND STATUS'.

Mark Strom[5]

The potential for downside risk to companies who have CEOs with high levels of narcissism (prestige, power and vanity) is very high. As Mark Stein, professor of leadership and management at Leicester University in the UK, points out,

> One of the biggest problems with narcissistic managers is their extreme feelings of omnipotence and their deluded thinking that they can shift the market and know the future. As a consequence, and in the face of clear and stark warnings from others, they may take on extreme and unnecessary risks that endanger the future of the organisation.[6]

One well-known example of the risks and consequences of such leaders is Bernie Madoff. Madoff was very smart with finance. He'd helped to create the NASDAQ exchange and founded one of the most successful broker-dealers in the industry. He was highly respected for his achievements and philanthropy and as one-time vice-chairman of the National Association of Securities Dealers, his industry's own watchdog. But only a small group in the industry discovered that he also ran and controlled his own hedge fund to funnel money from investors into his broker-dealer, Bernard L. Madoff Investment Securities (BLMIS). A small group of analysts led by Harry Markopolis[7] could not believe the returns being made by BLMIS based on stock market returns. Markopolis gathered evidence for Madoff's Ponzi Scheme (using new investment money to pay interest to other investors rather than making real investments). Markopolis provided the evidence to the SEC (the New York Stock Exchange regulator) in May 2000. But amongst all the smart people, no one would listen and no one could believe that Madoff could carry off such a fraud.

Markopolis kept on the trail until the fraud was exposed in December 2008 as the largest-ever Ponzi scheme in history. By its end, Madoff had effectively stolen $17.5bn from more than 4,000 BLMIS account holders as well as from thousands more third-party investors exposed through feeder funds. Madoff confessed to his sons that it was 'all just one big lie'. He was jailed for 150 years in July 2009.

In the London High Court recovery proceedings related to Madoff's London trading operation, Madoff's London directors described him variously as 'aggressive', a 'wild man' and a 'control freak'. John Purcell, who worked in Madoff's London office for almost 13 years until 2001, said under cross-examination, 'I've seen him [Madoff] being a hell of a bully, a terrible bully, and tear a broker's throat out who worked for us.'[8] The reasons for Madoff's paranoia for secrecy are now clear but it is sad that a man who started a tiny brokerage in 1960 with US$5,000 of capital and office space borrowed from his father-in-law should end up with a list of obsessive-compulsive behaviours being declared in a London court as a result of the paranoia and stresses of his great 'success'.

Newspapers have made much of the lavish lifestyle enjoyed by Madoff, mentioning his beachfront mansion in the Hamptons, a villa overlooking Cap d'Antibes in the South of France, and yachts in New York, Florida and the Mediterranean. The press focuses on the point that Madoff's lifestyle was funded at the expense of new entrants to his fund. There is nothing wrong with owning beautiful homes and yachts but when the Suit demands their acquisition whatever the human and ethical cost, most people are outraged.

In the organisational context, good senior leaders who have acted with integrity can find success and a privileged position results in a sudden increase in the Gap. Some ethical studies have found that successful people can lose focus and obtain largely unconstrained control and privilege over organisational resources, developing an almost magical belief in their own ability to manipulate outcomes and therefore to conceal their wrongdoing.[9]

We can readily point to public figures who could be described as 'smart', ultimately discovering that they were foolish. But the potential for foolishness, narcissism, paranoia and self-deception lies in us all. Sometimes we over-estimate our smartness and that leads to foolishness. The Monk simply guides us to live happily with ourselves and those around us and is not over-concerned with 'smartness'. The bigger the Gap between the conscience of our inner self, our Monk, and the ego drives of our Suit, the greater the risk of foolish and / or unethical behaviours and decisions.

Thankfully there are many great examples of business leaders who seem to have aligned their Suit with their Monk and hold power lightly. Bill Gates has given more and more of his role away at Microsoft and is now fully dedicated to the expansive and world changing work of the Bill & Melinda Gates Foundation. The world's most respected investor, Warren Buffet, also seems to be free of any need to project himself beyond a relatively modest lifestyle for a man of wealth, most of which he has donated to the Bill & Melinda Gates Foundation. Nobel Peace Laureate, Muhammad Yunus, has been an example of social business entrepreneurship which he says is dedicated to solve problems, not to make personal money.[10]

There is nothing particularly wrong with the Suit (or Suits) that we wear for the external world. The risks to our personal happiness, and possibly the happiness of others too, arise when our Suit is unchecked by the sense and perception of our Monk. In other words, we find our Suit causing us to overplay who we really are. There is nothing wrong in highlighting our achievements and our strengths but the internal gap is enlarged when we exaggerate or feel we have to add something more to who we really are. We become inauthentic and, over time, inauthentic claims and behaviours are sensed by the Monks in people around us. It may not be obvious at first, but the Gap can become larger or smaller depending on the choices you make and the way you manage yourself.

Suit-Monk Awareness

Many of us are unaware of the Gap that exists in our lives. Lacking this awareness may have caused problems in developing our values and our talents. We may have tried different techniques to move on from a position of dissatisfaction. If you are not aware of the Gap, then self-development tends to be largely Suit-work. This means that you work on techniques, goals and skills to boost your self-confidence and to project yourself more fully into the place that you would like to be.

So, how can we develop the Monk in ourselves and amongst those we lead? In the chapters that follow we aim to answer that question by applying the Suited Monk concept and explaining how we can tackle the Gap that can occur between our Suit and our Monk. The starting point is self-awareness – knowing yourself at a deeper level.

Are you ready to take the journey with us?

1. Mandela, N., 1995, *Long Walk to Freedom,* Macdonald Purnell, 1994, Johannesburg.

2. Lance Armstrong and Oprah Winfrey: interview transcript: http://www.bbc.co.uk/sport/0/cycling/21065539

3. Bill George, 2011, "Why leaders lose their way", *HBR Blog Network.* Source: http://blogs.hbr.org/hbsfaculty/2011/06/why-leaders-lose-their-way.html

4. Sternberg, R. J., 2004, "Why Smart People Can Be So Foolish", *European Psychologist,* Vol. 9, No. 3, September 2004, pp. 145–150.

5. Reproduced by kind permission of Mark Strom from his book: *Lead with Wisdom,* John Wiley, Melbourne, 2014, p.195.

6. Quoted by Naomi Shragai in "Life with a narcissistic manager", *Financial Times,* 28 October, 2013.

7. Harry Markopolis tells the story of Bernie Madoff in: *No One Would Listen: A True Financial Thriller,* (John Wiley, Hoboken, NJ, 2010).

8. Madoff Securities International Ltd. v. Raven, 10-1468, High Court of Justice, Queen's Bench Division (London), June 2013.

9. Robert A. Prentice finds evidence that the types of people who become top corporate officers and the settings in which they find themselves can combine to create unusual susceptibility to committing ethical errors in "Good directors and bad behavior", *Business Horizons* (2012) 55, 535-541.

10. Yunus, M., 2014, speaking at the World Economic Forum in the panel on the "Future of Capitalism".

2. SELF-REALISATION

I have often thought that the best way to define a person's character would be to seek out the particular mental or moral attitude in which, when it came upon them, they felt themselves to be most deeply and intensively active and alive. At such moments, there is a voice inside which speaks and says, "This is the real me".

William James, 1878[1]

Knowing yourself is the personal quest both to realise your full potential and to understand more about the essence of your character, beliefs, values and personality. Knowing yourself is measured by the level of self-awareness you have. Leaders with high self-awareness usually have less ego and are more open and collaborative and usually bring more passion to work. Becoming such a leader involves allowing your Monk to show through your Suit and align your Suit with your Monk – this is called authentic leadership.

Bill George, the former President of Medtronic, identifies five reasons for leadership failure:[1]

- Lack of self-awareness
- Unwilling to face failure
- Seeking external gratification
- Unwilling to seek advice
- No balance in life

These same reasons are also the causes of what we call burnout. Burnout is the experiencing of chronic stress in which a person is left in a state of depression, with little energy and motivation and overwhelmed by mental, emotional and physical exhaustion. Burnout can be brought on not only by overwhelming demands being made on us but by overarching fears for our future, or our family's future, amidst the challenges of living and leading in a VUCA world. Leaders in midlife on the journey of their career are particularly vulnerable to depression or burn-out, sometimes feeling locked in to their circumstances with no way out but to stick to the path they have been treading for many years. The Gap has become too big to manage: people suffer in their jobs, have no time for their children and family and live a life that is not true to them-selves and does not nurture their Monk.

The two charts below illustrate in a very simple way the Suit-Monk Gap. If people self-realise and their Suit and Monk are aligned, then leadership authenticity emerges.

If there is no alignment then burnout or leadership failure are the likely result.

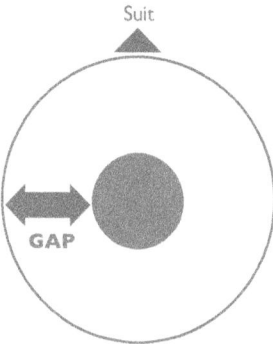

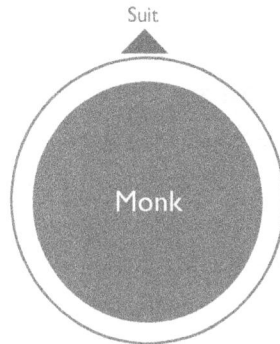

How do I self-realise?

Self-realisation is a journey that is unique to you. In your career, external opportunities will come, or may not, but it's only your decision that will decide the course of your career. Your life circumstance today is a result of the decisions that you have made in the past. So, if you are not fulfilled in your job it's because of your past decisions. That choice may not have been in harmony with who you really are as a person. If that's the case, then you have two choices for the future: trust or fear.

Your first step is to be willing to change. Reading this book is one way to help you to raise awareness about the bigger picture of life, career and purpose. Once your awareness has been raised and you are open to change, then you have to ask yourself: what's next? Any question that you ask yourself can be answered by your Suit or your Monk. Those choices will determine the direction of your life and career. If the Suit is not aligned with the Monk then people tend to express fear, avoid facing reality, and are focused on personal gain and rational outcomes. When choices are based on a person's Monk then they become capable of reflection, trust and acting with courage; they will also adapt to change more easily.

Self-realisation does mean 'time out' for yourself - what we call Monk Time. Monk Time is when you take 'time out of time' from the external world, your work, your home-life demands and your expectations to just be with yourself. In that time frame do something that nurtures yourself, read a book, enjoy time on your own in a coffee shop or go for a walk in a peaceful environment, take a day off to go to a mountain, the coast, or ski. You may already find that there are opportunities to make Monk Time from simple physical tasks that can trigger an alternative state of mind like washing your car. In Mike's case his Monk Time is often spent doing garden work when his Monk gets refreshed even though his body gets tired! When you create Monk Times in your week you will notice that you return' to the external world refreshed and recharged with new ideas and insights. In Monk Time the mind is quiet and the Monk is nurtured. We also invite you to schedule some Monk Time and an activity for purely yourself in your weekly calendar.

Another way to develop self-realisation is through

practising mindfulness. Bill George says that mindful leadership

> …teaches you to pay attention to the present moment, recognizing your feelings and emotions and keeping them under control, especially when faced with highly stressful situations. When you are mindful, you're aware of your presence and the ways you impact other people. You're able to both observe and participate in each moment, while recognizing the implications of your actions for the longer term. And that prevents you from slipping into a life that pulls you away from your values.[2]

When you are mindful you are not attached to outcomes, you are an observer of outcomes. You are not attached to expectations, you observe expectations. You basically become an observer of your mind, your life, your colleagues and your company. In that space of observing you have an ability to look at more possibilities and more opportunities. If you are not good at listening to others, mindfulness will help you to take a step back and not be attached to your own beliefs and the responses you want to give. You allow and give space to the other person to share his/her points of view without judgement. Mindfulness will also reduce pressure on your Suit, because you can observe your beliefs and question them. When you are mindful you look beyond your Suit and you operate from within yourself. There are some basic mindfulness techniques that you can use each day set out in the Practising Mindfulness box at the end of this chapter.

The benefits of mindfulness practice are being recognised in the growing number of personal development programmes used by companies. Ford Motor Company chairman Bill Ford and former Google.org director, Larry Brilliant, are among executives who advocate mindfulness practice. Arianna Huffington, President and Editor-in-Chief of the Huffington Post Media Group has experienced the benefits of mindfulness practice: 'Stress-reduction and mindfulness don't just make us happier and healthier,' she says, 'they're a proven competitive advantage for any business that wants one.'[3] General Mills have offered a mindfulness programme for their employees since 2006. It was founded by Janice Marturano, General Mills' deputy general counsel who described mindfulness as 'training our minds to be more focused, to see with clarity, to have spaciousness for creativity and to feel connected.'[4]

The self-realisation of an entrepreneur

Peter Buytaert, co-founder of GLO – Good Leaders Online - is a Belgian who has worked in Asia for close to thirty years. In 2006, he left his job as President Agfa Graphics Asia to set up China Global Leaders, a management consultancy which successfully assisted more than twenty foreign invested and local start-ups in China, providing business modelling, mentoring and incubator support. Throughout his career Peter recognised the inner prompts of his Monk. 'It seemed to start when I was 12 years old,' he told us, when he instinctively felt that he would leave Belgium when he was older. We asked him to explain more: 'It was just a strong gut feeling that somehow spoke to me. I had no idea what career to pursue at that time so I started to study law as I believed that would enable me to leave the country as soon as possible and to wear the Suit of a diplomat.'

But at law school, Peter soon realised that he didn't like the bureaucracy and formality of law and so he quit to study international business. 'Although many of my friends and family thought quitting law school was a crazy idea, for me, it was the right thing to do. In hindsight my instinct turned out to be completely correct. At business school I developed a passion and an interest in the world of exports and entrepreneurship so I continued to follow the guidance of my Monk.'

Peter's opportunity to leave Belgium came by winning a Prince Albert Fellowship to work in Hong Kong for a year. From there he moved to join Agfa's medical division as a marketing manager. Like many in their early business careers, Peter worked hard and achieved material success and a good income. Why risk it? For Peter, earning well in a good career was not satisfying. Peter's entrepreneurial spirit was stifled by what he recalled was a highly bureaucratic and political environment.

At times in our career path, we have opportunities

presented to us that lift us up, or crises that can bring us down. For Peter, five years into his Japanese career with Agfa, he took stock of his position and recalls the dilemma he faced: 'Should I continue to pursue the material benefits for a job that was not in line with my soul? Or, should I take a risk and follow the energy of my heart? Suddenly my Monk started to remind me of my interest in being creative in the business context and I knew I had to find an opportunity where I could really build something from scratch which in my own way would feel satisfying for me.'

This powerful self-realisation was accompanied by an opportunity with a risk. Peter received a call from a business associate who invited him to become a business partner in a photoshop retailing business. 'I accepted the invitation because I believed it would meet my needs to express my creativity. It turned out that the values of the partners I was now working with were strongly out of alignment with my own which resulted in a stressful year full of struggle. I didn't enjoy the experience at all.' As a result the partnership failed and for a while Peter was brought down by feelings of failure, knowing that he and his wife, Chin, were unhappy with their environment for family life.

Feelings of failure are part of life's journey. We need to respond to what we may consider failures from our Monk's perspective. Our Monk is not tied into the immedi-ate events that cause such failings. Our Monk contains the unique DNA for our life purpose and is ready to prompt our mind with positive opportunities. The Monk perspective simply regards such failings as a learning experience to help us on our way. It is emotionally and psychologically difficult for us to respond positively when our emotions have been bruised. We have to take a little time to recover. Recovery time needs to be managed with the discipline not to allow our minds to fill us with depression and despair by worrying about the pressing realities of job and money. It can be very painful to wait actively for the next step to emerge.

It is not at all unusual for people to pursue a line of opportunity that they feel is strongly aligned to their gifts and talents only to find that the opportunity does not immediately open up for them. But the experience of pursuing an opportunity can lead to a heightened aware-ness of other opportunities that excite us. Leadership is about persistence, not a driven persistence of the ego, but rather a trusted vision and purpose from our Monk.

Peter rebounded and rejoined AGFA to start an office in Malaysia which offered him the entrepreneurial dimension he was looking for. 'From Kuala Lumpur, we set up new distributors in S.E. Asia and opened an office in Vietnam. Then they asked me to go to Korea and China and to become head of Asia. But the politics, as is common in many larger organisations, kicked in again and very soon I was like a fish on dry land. I had been in the comfort zone for seven years and decided to take a big leap of faith to set up my own consultancy in China.'

Peter continued his life journey in a new business world of his own creation. He followed his heart and responded to challenges from within, as the story above illustrates. Like many of us, Peter developed a career but increasingly found the career path unrewarding in terms of true joy and purpose in life. In the episodes from Peter's story there are two periods in which he reflected about his vocation, deepened his self-awareness and found a fresh energy arising to pursue a new career path. We call this the journey towards self-realisation which involves a gradual awakening of your real self, your Monk, to see that your existence does not have to be solely determined by the external world. Self-realisation is usually close to a period of suffering, described by Peter as being like a fish on dry land. The experience of self realisation rises up from within and is usually an internal battle as your Monk calls out to you and reminds you of your unique identity and gifts and points to a potential new life adventure.

Peter's Gap

Peter's Suit Before
Law Study
Bureaucratic culture
Corporate Environment
Suit
Monk
Fish on dry land

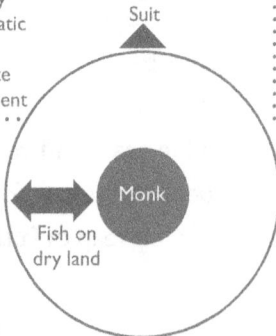

Peter's Suit After:
Entrepreneur
Investor
Start-Up
Innovative Culture
Suit
Risk taking
Entrepreneurial
Adventurous
Independent

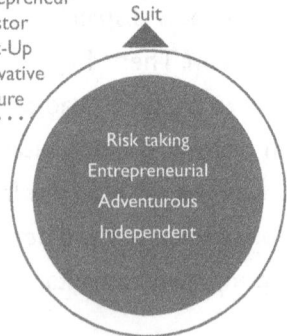

The self-realisation of a CEO

For Richard Evans, as Chief Executive of InBev UK in 2008, the jolt came to leave a career in corporate life at the age of 42. He realised that he had money but little joy in his business life, and little space for anything but the business he served. The safe and logical career next step for Richard would have been to move on to another CEO job based on his strong CV. But Richard's self-realisation led him to realise that there was something else he could do in business that would enable him to deploy his talents in a more purposeful way, whilst creating space to find joy in his personal life alongside this. Finding a new career or life journey path when you have been a known and successful business leader is not as easy as you may think. Once you step away from your career-based network you can feel quite lonely. We have experienced these points in our past career journeys. But your Monk helps you to reach out to new people and you make new friends who come to you as you set out to explore the possibilities. For Richard it took about a year for him to transition to a fulfilling 'portfolio career' which enabled him to make a purposeful social contribution to wider society. He now chairs the boards of School-Home Support, a London-based educational charity for children from disadvantaged backgrounds, Hub King's Cross, a London social entrepreneurship network, and Envero, a brand consultancy focused on helping mainstream brands and companies build greater trust with their customers.

Richard describes his journey from the corporate world as a freedom to become who he really is as a person. He still works with the challenges associated with managing businesses (and a charity) in tough economic conditions but he now operates from a deeper place of wellbeing. The journey of life continues for Richard but he faces challenges differently now, with a greater sense of purpose, acceptance, and a readiness to incorporate intuitive insights into the business facts.

The self-realisation that you are in the right job

Isabel Bi* participated in one of Raf's workshops and described how she had been offered a job with another company but was not sure about whether she should take the opportunity. Isabel would have had to relocate to Shanghai from Guangzhou, at a higher level and a higher salary. It was only after attending Raf's workshop that Isabel connected with her Monk and realised how much she loved her current job. She loved her colleagues and she loved living in Guangzhou. It was only by realising the passion and voice of her Monk that she could make the decision to stay in her current job, rather than to be enticed by her Suit to a position that might have led her in the wrong direction for her career and happiness.

---

* Not her real name.

Often people receive invitations from headhunters for job opportunities that seem better than what they currently have. But a better job offer doesn't necessarily mean a better job or more happiness. Just because you have some issues currently with your spouse doesn't mean that you have to file for divorce and find someone else. Sometimes you have to use difficulties and challenges as the means for growth as a couple. This analogy can be carried over into your career as well. In business you need to consider questions such as: Do I enjoy my work? Do I like being with my colleagues? Here the challenges are opportunities for learning and growth.

From time to time it's very important to stand still and reflect. Where am I on my life journey? Am I on a path towards my personal passion and purpose? Does my work give me opportunities to learn and grow towards the next step in my life? Learn to see your current job as a learning opportunity to cultivate both your Monk and your Suit. As long as both are in alignment and they are growing and developing with the joy of the Monk as driver, happiness will remain. Challenging situations happen in every job. As long as you can work with the challenges and overcome those because your Monk is the main driver you can enjoy the journey of your life and career.

Your Life Journey

Raf has displayed the Life Journey as a journey that can follow one of two choices: the Ego or Suit choice or the Spirit or Monk choice (see the Life Journey Model at the back of the book). Over time, the internal journey of the Spirit/Monk becomes deeper and brings fulfilment and reward throughout our life.

We believe that to realise one's life purpose our Suit and our Monk have to work in harmony. At birth, Suit and Monk are in harmony but the socialisation process usually pushes towards a separation between our Suit and our Monk. We want to look good in our Suit but are often less clear to hear the voice of our Monk. As we have already suggested, this separation is the Gap between a person's external world being the life they are living and the inner world which is the life that they really want.

In the work context, many can feel that they are in jobs that cultivate the Suit but which don't nurture their Monk. Ideally the Gap is reduced so that you can live a life and career with purpose and be successful at the same time. Once your Suit and Monk are aligned, the Gap shown by the two choice lines of the Life Journey model disappears and Suit and Monk are aligned in the external world. The more you close the Gap, the more the Monk choice line will move upwards. Usually when that happens, monetary success becomes a by-product because your life purpose will drive you forward.

Peter, Richard and Isabel chose to trust their Monk and so the path and flow of life were revealed to them in the career decisions they made. Peter and Richard decided to change their whole line of work to self-realise while Isabel found renewed fulfilment and energy by realising the joy of her current work. If there was no fear, what decision would you make right now for your life, career and family? Would you make any changes? If you sense a 'yes' from your heart, then that is the voice from within and that voice is helping you to realise yourself.

We can have many self-realising experiences in our lives, perhaps due to a life or career crisis, or maybe during a prolonged period of stress. It's as though the external world jolts our internal world so strongly that we see things with new eyes – a new layer of perception and hope opens up to us. The opportunity is for our Suit to be better moulded around our Monk through a fresh life departure from a past way of living or working.

Life Rewards

Life rewards come to you when you follow your purpose and your path. Every step you take that brings you closer to your purpose will most likely be accompanied by true happiness: the joy of doing what you love (like Isabel), a greater sense of awareness (of yourself and of others) and a freedom and confidence in going with the flow of life. We do not lightly say this, but we believe that life's reward can include being happy every day at a deep level. It's a feeling of deep contentment about yourself, your life, your job and your relationships. Life rewards arise from a deep understanding of yourself, and they accompany the internal journey (not the external journey) which brings fulfilment on a daily basis. You are simply entering into a state of active contentment or peacefulness.

You might worry that you will lose your life rewards after you finally receive them, just as you lost happiness at other times in your life. But if you find your purpose, and receive life's rewards, they will stay with you. The more you keep practicing acceptance, using your intuition in decision making and discovering your purpose in life, the more the Gap closes, which is the subject of the next chapter. Happiness increases and so the rewards will stay with you for a lifetime because your spirit keeps growing and it's the growth of your spirit that brings such rewards. You may well feel that living only for each day is not wise in planning for your future life security. But, living and enjoying your day today does not mean that responsible planning should not be part of your day. The question is: do you worry about your future security now? Jesus did not lightly say 'do not worry about tomorrow, for tomorrow will worry about itself.' He said these words to his followers because he was asking them to raise their vision to seek the higher road of his kingdom first, in other words to put first things first.[5] We can have a taste of this kind of living by trusting our Monk to guide us and to sense the flow of life and the environment in which we live and work at a higher level.

Our future in the external world is a mental projection of ever-extending ourselves unrealistically to a VUCA world of 'more, better, faster.' Sometimes we face unrealistic goals that result in suffering (the feelings of discontentment) which end up blurring or even destroying our life in the present. You may tell yourself that you'll be happier in the future, that you'll have a better job, home, or relationship. You plan, plot, and strategise, but unfortunately you don't find the inner peace and contentment you crave. You focus on the possibility of future calamities and you become preoccupied by the 'what if' scenarios: what if I lose my job, suffer an illness, or experience a natural disaster? Your work and life evolves one step at a time. Each step will guide you towards the right direction in the future on a personal level and professional level.

In the end, we are all on an individual journey of self-realisation with its unique story. For Peter it was to become an entrepreneur and make some difficult choices. For Richard, it was leaving his corporate job to become the chair of the board of School-Home Support in London, leading an Impact Hub, and joining Envero. For all of us, change and challenge is inevitable and we have to make our choices each day. Sometimes it's time to move on, time to evolve and to grow to the next level. You can choose to operate and live from your mind or slowly start to embrace your Monk and learn to listen to your heart.

The more you listen to your heart, the more flow will come into your life and the easier your life will become. Sometimes rational decisions or outcomes seem ideal but allow your Monk to have a say in every decision. Allow logic and intuitive insight to go hand in hand in all your future decisions.

Self-realisation means allowing yourself to take control of your life, not by forceful mental determination, but by a growing inner belief that you can keep going to the next step, going beyond what you can currently see for yourself by the internal energy that comes from your Monk. Watch for internal observations to emerge at any time. We find life insights coming to us at unexpected times and situations.

Self realisation leads to authentic leadership

Can you imagine your team being re-energised and passionate about their work? If you have benefitted from self-realisation and greater self awareness, you will naturally show this to your team. Self awareness enables you to accept your limitations and to admit them to yourself and others. But you can also grow in true confidence of your talent area. A number of research studies have shown that those who demonstrated a more accurate conception of their own skills, abilities, and preferences tended to perform better than those with a less accurate self-conception.[6]

When you are self aware you are more likely to attract and recruit good people to your team and will not be threatened if they are better than you. When Mike worked as an Operations Director for UK toy retailer, The Entertainer:

> *I was very aware that the people who reported to me were actually more expert and talented in their domains of people management and retail operations than I was. Over a five year period I gave more and more of my responsibilities away to others and helped to recruit specialists. At the end of that period I had given away my job to others. If you enjoy helping people succeed then don't worry about giving your work away to others – you'll continue to grow and life will bring new opportunities to you.*

1. William James, *The Letters of William James* (Boston: The Atlantic Monthly Press, 1920). Adjusted for inclusive language.

2. George, W., 2010, *Instructor's guide for authentic leadership development*, Harvard Business School Course Overview Notes for Instructors, p.10

3. George, W., 2012, "Mindfulness Helps You Become a Better Leader", *HBR Blog Network*, 26 October. Source: http://blogs.hbr.org/2012/10/mindfulness-helps-you-become-a/

4. Arianna Huffington, 2013, "Mindfulness, Meditation, Wellness and Their Connection to Corporate America's Bottom Line", *HuffPost Blog*, 18 March. Source: http://www.huffingtonpost.com/arianna-huffington/corporate-wellness_b_2903222.html

5. The General Mills mindfulness programmes and similar programmes by Target, Google, Aetna, Green Mountain Coffee Roasters, First Direct and Taj Hotels were reported in "The Mind Business" by David Gelles in *FT Magazine*, 24 August, 2012. Source: http://www.ft.com/cms/s/2/d9cb7940-ebea-11e1-985a-00144feab49a.html#ixzz2MVASI0TD

6. The Bible: Matthew 6:33.

7. See references made by Thompson, R., 2014, "For a More Flexible Workforce, Hire Self-Aware People", *HBR Blog Network:* http://blogs.hbr.org/2014/01/for-a-more-flexible-workforce-hire-self-aware-people.

3. CLOSE THE GAP

I wound up withholding "the real me" from colleagues at work, coming across as super-confident, aggressive, and completely focused on business results. When I began sharing my weaknesses — being impatient, lacking tact, and often coming across as intimidating — as well as the failures and difficulties I had experienced in my lifetime, I learned that people opened up about themselves and resonated more with my leadership.
Bill George, former CEO of Medtronic[1]

When Bill George speaks of his 'real me' he is contrasting his Monk with the Suit's super-confident and aggressive performance. But he closed the Gap through being honest with himself and in his relationships with others acknowledging that his performance was not his 'real me.' Bill George aligned his Suit with his Monk.

The table below summarises the contrasting characteristics of a person whose Suit is not aligned with their Monk (a big Gap) and the person who lives with their Suit and Monk aligned: the Gap is small or non-existent and can be referred to as the 'Aligned Suit.'

Suit not aligned with Monk	Suit aligned with Monk
Rational decisions	Intuitive + Rational
Fear / Negative Beliefs	Courage / Trust
Resists change	Accepts change
Denial	Acceptance
Personal gain	Larger purpose
Projected Self	Self-realisation
Objectives and Plans	Flow
Profit	Purpose and Profit
Goal	Goal + Vision
Short Term	Short + Long term

To begin with, we believe that it is possible to close the Gap in your personal life and your work life by bringing your Suit and Monk into alignment. To help close the Gap we first need to master important two laws of life: the law of rejection and the law of acceptance. Understanding how these laws operate in your life will help you to close the Gap.

The Law of Rejection

Have you ever reacted emotionally when someone criticised you? Have you ever felt frustrated because you didn't get a promotion or job offer from a company? Have you ever remained upset because a customer cancelled a large sales order? Have you ever become defensive in meetings even if you were wrong? If the answer is yes, you may have inadvertently applied the law of rejection to yourself.

Rejection is the cause of stress. This is the law of rejection:

Whenever we reject something, whether it is an external situation or an internal feeling, a negative past emotion or state, we increase the Gap between our authentic self and the ego, between the heart and the mind, and between the Suit and the Monk. Whenever we reject or resist our current situation, we experience a greater personal struggle combined with feelings of stress, anger and frustration.

In a VUCA world, many undesirable and unforeseen events happen in business. We like to think we have control over ourselves and over these situations. This makes us feel safe, stable, and powerful. We may feel a sense of security, but we don't really have the degree of control we think we have. In meetings, for example, we resist and we reject input by others in an effort to gain and maintain control, but our efforts are in vain. We operate by instincts of habit and desires for comfort and so we naturally reject changes that loosen our control over a settled position or viewpoint. Even if opportunities accompany these events, we can still fear change and therefore reject it. As a result, we maintain or even increase the Gap within and lose opportunities for collaboration. Rejection is based in the ego and on deep-seated fears: fear of change, fear of failure in the taking on of a new assignment and the fear of rejection from others.

Rejection can also occur in our personal identity. When someone says something bad or negative about you at work your instinct is to take it personally and to react. You may become defensive because you think you will feel less worthy than if you don't. You are uncomfortable with what the person has said, but even more uncomfortable with the idea of not responding. In this way, you sustain the Gap within you.

External World - Rejection

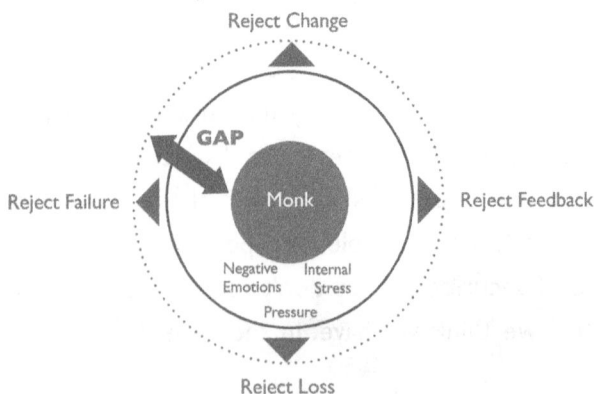

Often it is not a matter of outright rejection. It can be more subtle than that. Instead of a flat 'No!' you simply put up resistance. It's like erecting a wall around yourself because the resistance can continue for a long time and may even become your prevailing attitude. The more you resist the messages that come to your Suit (i.e. from the external world), the larger the Gap you will experience and the more you will feel pressure. This won't just create problems for you, it can also make things difficult for the people around you. They may find it hard to like and accept you and to collaborate with you. People are unlikely to appreciate you if you have built a wall around yourself that keeps them out. Sometimes you can reject the idea that you may have done something wrong; you push away the thought of wrongdoing and find ways to justify your actions. This is another way in which the law of rejection can work, by not facing up to a wrong decision or behaviour that deep down (in your Monk) you know to be wrong, you are rejecting the truth and so extending the Gap. When this happens, healing comes from facing the truth and admitting to yourself that your decision or behaviour was not right. Forgive yourself, embrace mistakes and let go of the offences that others have caused you. This is what it means to be strong. As Mahatma Gandhi said, 'The weak can never forgive. Forgiveness is the attribute of the strong.'

In the quotation from Bill George at the head of this chapter you can see that he reached a point in his career when he felt he had to come clean about his weaknesses, failures and difficulties. In his writing and speaking about authentic leadership he helps people see that mistakes and failures are valuable for learning. By embracing his mistakes and being open about them he says that people opened up about themselves and resonated more with his leadership.

In your family relationships and with your team members, admit when you are wrong. Say that you made a mistake and invite help towards any solutions required by the mistaken decision or action. When you go out to people who have been affected by your error with honesty and humility they may be initially upset, but generally you will get a constructive response. This level of acceptance and personal forgiveness is what personal integrity and humility really means. Becoming a person of character takes courage. Start with small steps and over a period of time you will see the difference in the way in which people will respond to you and follow your lead.

The Law of Acceptance

You may be wondering how you can overcome personal resistance and struggle, and how you can bridge the Gap within yourself. One primary step is to embrace the law of acceptance:

Whenever we accept something that we would normally fear or is beyond our control - whether it is an external situ-

ation or an internal feeling or state - we decrease the Gap.

As we can't control the external world, the wisest approach is to accept what happens to us. This does not mean giving up or becoming passive; it means recognising that the event, or circumstance, 'is what it is,' without resisting it or attributing additional meaning to it. In fact, it can involve taking an active stance and facing what is happening without judgement, and simply welcoming it.

External World - Acceptance

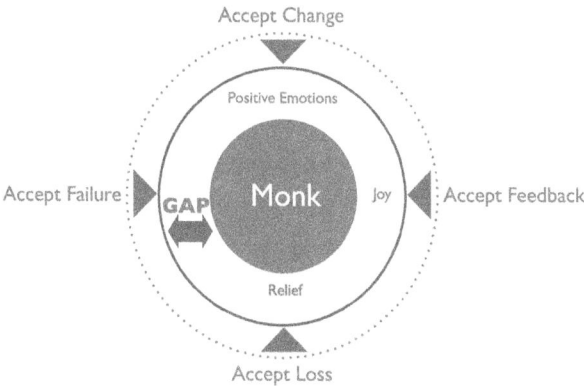

Accept Change

Positive Emotions

Accept Failure
GAP
Monk
Joy
Accept Feedback

Relief

Accept Loss

Sometimes life brings us challenges in big ways, and sometimes in smaller ways. Each challenge is an opportunity for growth. Whilst we can't escape what is happening now, or in the future, or in the past, we can change how we respond to what happens to us. In each moment we have an opportunity either to reject or to accept. Another way to look at this is to say that we can either become a victim of the incidents of life or take ownership of our lives and the incidents that occur. This means 'owning' who you are, what you stand for and what you believe in. Practising acceptance is a source of inner strength and enables us to follow the flow of life through us. We shall discuss the practice of acceptance further in chapter five.

Measuring Your Gap

Before you attempt to close the Gap, it is helpful to get a better sense of how your Gap currently manifests. The diagram below illustrates a personal Gap model. Responses (a) to (d) illustrate a Gap, arising from feelings and beliefs related to interactions in the external world. Responses (e) to (h) are issues that happen within you and which contribute to the size of your Gap.

Look at this diagram and think about how you interact in your Suit with the external world. Reflect on the questions that follow and see how they may apply to you.

External World

a. I am afraid to speak on stage (fear)

b. I don't think I am smart enough to be an entrepreneur (belief & fear of uncertainty)

c. I am stressed to meet my monthly company goals to satisfy all stakeholders

d. I try to live up to other people's expectations because I worry people may judge me for who I truly am

Ego / Suit

Fear   Beliefs

g. I feel **frustrated** because one of my colleagues made an unethical decision

GAP

i. Integrity
Monk
Personal Values
Talent/Potential
Wisdom
Purpose

e. I feel stress because I need to compromise on my personal values

f. I feel guilty for having taken a shortcut

h. I didn't help my friend when he needed me and I feel **shame**

1. Questions related to fears and beliefs (Suit): a. and b. in the Gap mode
- What fears are holding me back from reaching my full potential?
- What positive and negative beliefs do I hold?

2. Questions related to pressures: c. and d.
- What are the external changes that create pressure on my Suit?

3. Questions related to. emotions: e, f, g and h.
- How effectively do I manage my emotions and feelings?

4. Questions related to my inner Monk: i.
- Are there decisions I have made which have compromised my values?
- Have I made unethical shortcuts which make me feel guilty?
- How and when do I take time to listen to and nurture my inner Monk?

Read each of the following statements and ask yourself how accurately they describe you in your current day-to-day work?

- I am generally peaceful when facing uncertainty or during change.
- I know my values and don't compromise on them.
- I am aware of my purpose and how I express it in

my work.
- I use intuition in decision making.
- I look for mutual collaboration rather than personal gain.
- I lead with integrity and care, even if I have to sacrifice personal gain.
- My work and life are integrated.

As you reflect on these questions, do you find that you have a better overall sense of the extent to which the Gap shows up in your life? If all the statements bulleted above currently ring true then you are probably comfortable with yourself and have learned how to deal with the external and internal worlds and your Gap is likely to be minimal. On the other hand, if the questions highlight an internal struggle, tension or painful external pressures without solutions then your Gap still needs to be closed. When you are able to close it, you will be more effective as a leader.

Ways to Close the Gap

The Gap indicates how self-aware you are in knowing yourself, your values, your purpose, but also how effective you are in life and in collaboration with others. The four ways you can close the Gap correspond to the four question groups above. Three of them relate to managing your Suit. The fourth nurtures your Monk. We shall explain each of the following four Gap-closing ways in turn:

1. Optimise how you manage your fears and beliefs (Suit)
2. Optimise the way you deal with external changes and external pressure.
3. Effectively manage your emotions and feelings.
4. Know your inner Monk to find your authentic self and learn to lead from within; discover personal integrity, make ethical choices for better self-management.

Each way shows you how to work from the inside out, coming from a 'place' beyond the mind (more on this in the next chapter). Each way requires practice, just as you would practice regularly to exercise and to keep fit. When the 'muscle' of your Monk is exercised and strengthened in the way you manage yourself and in making decisions, it transforms from a weak 'spirit' into a powerful source of leadership. The Suit and Monk are then eventually aligned when the well-exercised inner self has become like a guiding compass and the Suit is used as a tool to help you to make better decisions.

The way you manage your Suit is very personal. It is based on past experiences which create your current beliefs about yourself and others, and your environment and the external factors which influence your decisions (dealing with change).

Managing your Suit is a choice. Stress is not something that happens to us but the way we choose to respond to external challenges. If a customer is unhappy, some of us stay calm and try to find solutions, while others become anxious and concerned at the prospect of losing the client.

Your Suit is not who you are, it is a perception of your self. As a perception, it can be changed. In other words your Suit can be managed and brought into line with your Monk. Your Suit can be managed so that you can reduce responses to external challenges which have a negative effect on yourself and on others. How does your Suit react to challenges? Does it go quiet and withdraw, or, is it easily angered? Or maybe you are generally happy with the way your Suit responds to life's circumstances.

You can manage your Suit's responses to challenges and pressures by working on the Law of Acceptance. But there are also four practices that we recommend to help you to manage your Suit.

(i) Pause and suspend judgement
(ii) Practice observing your Suit
(iii) Check your expectations
(iv) Embrace your mistakes

(i) Pause and suspend Judgement

Sometimes we can find ourselves acting without stopping to reflect on what we really want to say or do.

It's as if we are on automatic pilot, just saying the first thing that comes to our mind, and reacting based on our initial emotions and thoughts. Some of the time, this might not seem to matter. But when something unexpected happens, or when other people have strong feelings or opinions, our knee-jerk reactions can create problems. The Suit has a fast capability for self-defence and attack if it feels threatened by a viewpoint that conflicts with its own. When this happens, the Monk is left out and a neutral constructive conversation isn't possible.

The practice of pausing is valuable because it gives you a chance to observe your Suit's responses and the responses of your colleagues in a neutral way. As you can see from the Gap diagram below, the key to this practice is to pause for a few seconds after an external event occurs. Before you react to the situation, wait two or three seconds - not a long pause that other people will notice. This is a quick and subtle adjustment of perception.

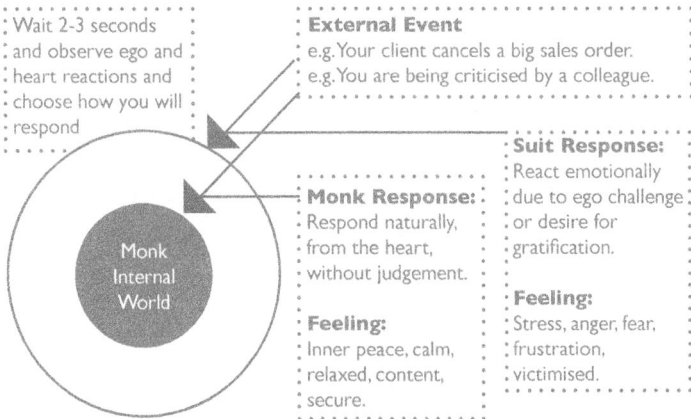

Wait 2-3 seconds and observe ego and heart reactions and choose how you will respond

External Event
e.g. Your client cancels a big sales order.
e.g. You are being criticised by a colleague.

Monk Internal World

Suit Response:
React emotionally due to ego challenge or desire for gratification.

Monk Response:
Respond naturally, from the heart, without judgement.

Feeling:
Stress, anger, fear, frustration, victimised.

Feeling:
Inner peace, calm, relaxed, content, secure.

In the fleeting but significant pause, 'space' is created between your Suit and your Monk, your mind and heart. The space that is created is what we call self-awareness. In this space of self-awareness, you become an observer of your own self.

You can observe your thoughts, your viewpoints, your beliefs and the emotions related to your initial reaction to a situation, a question or a comment. Observe the conversation and the behaviours of those around you. Be especially aware of people who seem to be communicating from their Suit. It is important that you suspend judgement. As an observer you adopt the position of neutral party who observes his or her Suit. There is great power in this state of suspended judgement because it keeps you from saying or doing things which you may later regret as you consider how best to respond.

This is a practice which means that you have to commit to do it and note if you failed to pause at times when it would have helped. Like practicing any new skill, in the beginning it might feel odd because you are not used to it but the more you practice, the more easily you will be able to respond to situations and connect with people at Monk level. In a fast-moving environment when we all have plenty to say, this is a personal discipline. Be ready during your next relevant and challenging communication to use the pause practice. Try it when you next receive criticism

(ii) Practice observing your Suit

Observing your Suit is a related skill to pausing and suspending judgement. We all have a social identity that involves adjusting ourselves so we can engage in positive social relations. But the ego can squeeze our social self into a false mould that is not aligned with our true self. The false mould is a major source of inner tension and stress. Our mind has to work very hard to keep up what is actually a false identity as Lance Armstrong's drugs story shows. If we can observe the pretence happening then we have the chance to choose whether and how we rein in the false identity and allow our true self to be expressed in the situation.

Daniel Zhou, a rising-star shoe retail entrepreneur had worked hard to establish a shoe chain of twenty stores in Guangdong province in China. Daniel had fostered a loyal management team but he frequently could not understand how they could not see failings in the business in the way that he could. If his team were involved in negotiating a supplier contract, he would usually intervene as he was sure that he would spot a negotiating opportunity that they could not.

By nature Daniel had a volatile temperament and his wife was helping him to be more reasonable in his expectations of people. Daniel was often angry with subordinates who didn't appear to pull their weight. He would expect people to work beyond their normal hours whether or not they really needed to. As far as Daniel was concerned, there was always more work to be done. He was ambitious and was continually frustrated by what he felt were unambitious members of his management team.

Daniel was regularly losing his temper in an open office and in these situations he would listen to no one - everyone had to do exactly what he wanted. But Daniel could also be charming and genuinely cared for the welfare of his staff. He wished he could become more balanced in his temperament but was resigned that he could never change and that his anger was just part of his personality.

Daniel was aware of his behaviours so he was able to work on improving himself and increasing his self awareness. He practiced at listening to others and reflecting on how he had managed difficult conversations. Actually Daniel's Monk taught Daniel's Suit how to control his frustrations and to let through the care that he genuinely felt towards people. Often convincing people to change their behaviour doesn't work because they are not aware of it or ignorant of the need to change. Once someone is aware, however, they can identify their reactions towards others and observe their Suit.

Observing your Suit allows you to make better decisions because you look beyond your personal thinking to the larger picture. As you become an observer of your own reactions you then have the chance to change your thinking and approach towards difficult situations and difficult relationships. You will find yourself considering what is in the best interests of all when you make a decision and not just what is best for you.

As an exercise, try to reflect on your behaviours after you leave a meeting in which a conflict occurred. Try to reflect on whether your responses and behaviours demonstrated the best version of yourself. If not, you have witnessed your projected self (Suit). Ask yourself how you would behave differently in the future, applying more behaviours to be more true to yourself (Monk).

(iii) Check your expectations

Karen had been recently promoted from a head-quarters position in Shanghai to a regional field position. Instead of managing a few clients, she now had to manage a region. When she was working in the headquarters the people with whom she worked were very fast thinking and intelligent. She was able to push the team forward and able to achieve significant business success. But the team members in the region were less capable and less ambitious than her previous headquarters team. They needed more time to learn new skills and also complained that they didn't get enough resources from headquarters to succeed.

Initially Karen went to the new region with the same expectations and management style that she had in her headquarters role but the team in the region were less capable of driving business locally. There was a Gap between Karen's expectations and the capability of the team.

When you are leading a team you can only bring the team to the next level based on the team's capabilities and awareness. In Karen's case she had to be self-aware to see that the current team's ability was lower then the head-quarters team. She had to lower her expectations for the team because their level of self awareness and skill were not at the level to meet her expectations.

When you try to help someone to become more self-aware you have to move gradually and work within their current window of reality. This is the power of coaching, which enables the coachee to gradually raise new layers of self awareness one step at a time. If the Gap is too big or the expectations are too high then people burn out or become demotivated.

It is important to understand the relationship between your expectations and the Gap. Having strong expectations means that you will project a certain desired outcome. That then starts to become a factor in how you feel. On a personal level, for example, you might think: 'If I get that promotion, I shall be happy; if I don't get it, I shall be unhappy.' In this way, your expectations of the external world determine your happiness and unhappiness. If your expectation is not met, the Gap increases. If you work in sales and you expect to get the contract with the client and the client doesn't give it to you then your expectations are dashed and you won't be happy. In Daniel's case he was ambitious and was continually frustrated by what he felt were unambitious members of his management team. Daniel was regularly losing his temper and had to find a way to manage his Suit's reactions.

But he also had to tackle his expectations of people.

One way of dealing with expectations that disappoint is to manage the emotions in relation to their outcome. If your expectations are not realised, you accept that. Let the disappointment and emotions go and move on. You don't allow your Suit to dwell on the result or to work up feelings of anger or hurt.

Similarly, if you are leading a team, analyse your expectations with the capabilities of the team members. If your expectations of others are too high and they don't deliver or perform to meet your standards, both of you may feel frustrated. Instead, focus on helping people grow from within and become more self-aware. Look out for the joy that they bring in trying their best which will often outweigh any mistakes they might make.

As well as checking your expectations about major life events, such as career directions or relationship decisions, you can check expectations moment-by-moment.

In the VUCA world change is volatile and unexpected; we can become very uncomfortable with the fear, uncertainty and ambiguity that change brings. If you go with your immediate feeling and reaction, notice what happens to your Gap. But if you pause and check your expectations and attachments, you will realise that change is an inevitable event. Your best option is to accept the situation. Naturally you expect to be on time for a meeting but if you're running late due to a traffic jam, call the people involved and explain. There is no good reason to let the situation affect your inner state. In fact, most outcomes in the external world are beyond your control anyway, so why become attached to them?

iv. Embrace your mistakes

Sometimes you can reject the idea that you may have done something wrong – you push away the thought of wrongdoing and find ways to justify your actions. This is another way in which the law of rejection can work. By not facing up to a wrong decision or behaviour that deep down (in your Monk) you know to be wrong, you are rejecting the truth and thus extending the Gap. When this happens, face the truth and admit to yourself that your decision or behaviour was not right. Embrace your mistake and forgive yourself first.

Although forgiveness is normally an action that you give towards someone else, self-forgiveness is part of the law of acceptance in which you accept your failing and let go of the consequences of an action that you admit to have been wrong. Self-criticism needs to be managed wisely, as self-learning rather than as self condemnation. Self-criticism should be realistic and constructive. It should involve being able to see your shortcomings but also realising your gifts and the situations in which you really flow with your gifts.

As you become increasingly aware of your Suit and

you observe your Suit from within you are in a stronger position to make wise decisions and close the Gap. The reason for this is that you detach yourself from making judgments that are solely related to your own self interests. Wise people have a capacity to empathise with others and to act for a good that is beyond their self-interest. We shall discuss this further in chapter nine. Of course, our survival instinct directs us to take care of ourselves and our families first and our Monk and our Suit can be perfectly aligned with that aim. But even in survival mode we can go out towards others in kindness, respect and care. Perhaps you have experienced the generosity of people who may have little in a material sense but live richly with the life that they have. This was evident to Mike during a visit he made in 2011 to a slum area in Navotas City in Manila, The Philippines. Despite the tiny living quarters, densely populated living quarters and narrow walkways, some of which were extended over seawater, there was an order and happiness amongst the people. Everyone was smiling and friendly despite the evident daily struggles of existence. Children played happily, older ones looking after younger ones and no one begged for money. Mike was profoundly touched by witnessing such happiness within a community which might have otherwise been regarded as unhappy. Despite the hardships of the external world for these people, the Monks of their inner worlds were shining.

For those of us with more work to do on Gap

closure the rewards for aligning our Suit with our Monk
are illustrated in the diagram below.

Outcomes

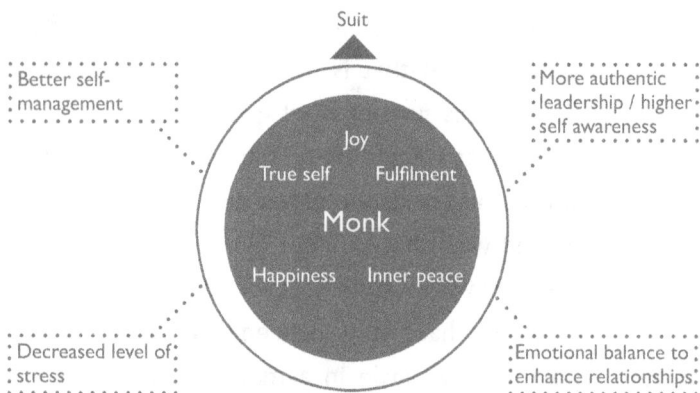

How do you feel today about where you are in life?
On a scale of 1 to 10 do you feel passionate about what
you do and are your natural talents nurtured and
developed? Or have external pressures (education, money,
status) driven a Gap between where you are where you
would really like to be?

Having offered strategies for narrowing the Gap
and working with the Suit, in the next chapters we shall
explore how we can nurture our Monk.

1. Bill George in his Foreword to *Leadership and the Art of Struggle* by Steve Snyder (Barrett-Koehler Publishers, San Francisco, 2013, p.xii).

4. INTUITIVE DECISION-MAKING

The intuitive mind is a sacred gift and the rational mind is a faithful servant. We have created a society that honours the servant and has forgotten the gift.

Unknown[1]

The South African coin was spinning over a white table in a Lagos hotel. Fifteen pairs of eyes watched intently to see whether it would land heads or tails. 'Tails,' Mike declared, as the coin rattled down on the table. 'Share your feelings about that, Henry,' said Mike. 'Disappointed,' replied Henry Obike, who was then head of E-Product Sales for the United Bank for Africa.

It was June 2013 and Mike had just finished a session on 'Wise Management' with a group of African alumni of China Europe International Business School (CEIBS) at the Eko Hotel in Lagos. In the Q&A Henry had asked how one can be sure to distinguish the inner voice of the heart from other voices. Mike had been describing the intuitive dimension of wisdom and the need to integrate intuitive insights ('sights' from within) with rational, fact-based thinking. He had told the group that our mental processes tend to suppress our heart-felt instincts often because of the risk and fear of the potential outcomes. Fear of uncertainty, fear of not being liked or approved and the fear of rejection. The more we develop the intuitive capacity, the more we discover the right path ahead as we apply our 'sixth sense'.

To answer Henry's question Mike asked him whether he could share a decision that he needed to make with the group – anything from his life that he would feel comfortable to share. Henry immediately responded by sharing a dilemma that he was facing in his career. He had to decide whether he would leave a job which he enjoyed, that was secure, and one in which he had been successful. Henry had been offered the chance to lead a new pan-African banking technology enterprise; he had been weighing up the pros and cons of leading a new venture. 'I'm concerned about leaving my colleagues at the bank – they pleaded with me not to leave when I had once considered leaving before.' The decision Henry had to make following a morning of phone calls on the subject was whether to leave his job for the new opportunity or not. Henry called it 'an internal struggle.' Mike said we would flip a coin on that choice.

'So, tell us your choice for heads or tails, Henry,' Mike said. 'Heads, I leave, tails, I stay,' he replied, as the mix of bankers, business people and psychologists looked on at this strange exercise.

The moment the coin was in the air, everyone was wondering on which side it would fall. We didn't know but it wasn't the outcome of the coin flip that was important. What was important was HOW Henry would respond. The coin landed on tails and the first response in Henry's body didn't look good. Mike was watching; Henry's shoulders bowed slightly, his eyes narrowed and his mouth showed disappointment. Henry's emotional response or gut feeling was his Monk 'speaking'. His heart was telling him that staying in his position was not the right thing to do and his body language showed this.

The coin allowed Henry to hear the true inner voice of his heart towards the choice he had to make. The decision was not to be based on a coin-flip. The coin flip was designed to reveal a deeper level of emotion or gut feeling about what his 'heart' really wanted. Henry was clearly impacted by the realisation that he wanted to go for the new career opportunity and he told us all that even when the coin was spinning he feared it would be tails. Henry's 'head' (rational planning processes) could now follow his heart. It is important to point out that only the immediate response to the result of the coin flip is significant in revealing the intuitive voice. Subsequent responses may be derived from fears projected in the mind and not actually your true intuitive voice. In February 2014, Henry told us:

> I found out that I needed to align my career path with the telecoms sector to achieve my ultimate dream of independence. I must confess that this has not been an easy choice for me to make but within me I somehow get so much conviction that I am now on the right path.

Reasonable Intuition

Don't we all 'sense' at some point that even though tough decisions have to be made, we simply know 'the right thing' to do? Ignoring intuitive insights leaves us exposed to the complexity of choices in the VUCA world which can so easily lead to indecisiveness. Intuition is needed in the VUCA world to help us with quality decision-making, visionary thinking and innovation. Intuition has a broad meaning and includes the idea of 'gut instinct'. It is an insight that naturally appears before the use of reason or the normal rational process of thought. Intuition is direct and effortless whereas brainpower logic can be hard work and lengthy.

Vidhu is the HR vice-president for a large pharma company in Asia-Pacific. Vidhu shared with us that at some point in his early career, a new job opportunity came along but his gut feel told him the values and culture did not sit right. Nevertheless, he decided to follow the attraction of monetary and job title rewards. Three months later, Vidhu had left his new employer. Even though all rationally processed information seems to be correct and to provide a holistic picture, you can still make the wrong decision. Intuitive power brings a different dimension to the decision-making process.

We recall one case in which a country GM was confronted with a hiring decision. His HR manager had supported a candidate for a strategic management position based on a thorough HR rational recruitment process. The GM, however, intuitively did not feel right. Nevertheless, based on the HR manager's professional recommendation, the candidate was offered the job. Within one year, however, the intuition proved right and the candidate was no longer with the company.

The need for intuition in financial markets

The global financial crisis (GFC) which began in 2008 was the result not only of greed but also of a high degree of reliance on risk-based models. One of these models is called Value at Risk (VaR), a widely used risk measure of the risk of loss on a specific portfolio of financial assets. During the years leading up to the GFC, the VaR model became very popular amongst securities traders as it is the only commonly used risk measure that can be applied to just about any asset class. VaR incorporates thousands of risk variables, including diversification, leverage and volatility, that make up the kind of market risk that traders and firms face every day. VaR answers the question, 'How much could my firm lose in a really bad month?' and the answer is presented as a percentage of the total investment based usually on a 95% or 99% level of confidence. In other words, 95 or 99 times out of 100 the firm would not lose more than a defined sum on a particular trading position.

Joe Nocera, writing in the New York Times during the crisis, pointed out that VaR did not measure the biggest risk of all: the possibility of a financial meltdown. He quoted David Einhorn, founder of Greenlight Capital, a prominent hedge fund manager, who wrote that VaR was 'relatively useless as a risk-management tool and potentially catastrophic when its use creates a false sense of security among senior managers and watchdogs. This is like an air bag that works all the time, except when you have a car accident.'[2] Risk-management models generally only covered data from the previous two decades, 'a period of euphoria' in the words of Alan Greenspan, former chairman of the US Federal Reserve.[3] Using risk-management models such as VaR also requires subjective judgments and insights and a consideration of the risks to other people.

The tale of the last minute salvation of the US financial system in 2008 is now well-known. A US government bail-out of $800 trillion was injected at the last minute to save the US and the world from a liquidity crisis. Freddie Mac, Fanny Mae, AIG, Citibank, Wells Fargo, Bank of America were saved and Lehman and Bear Stearns were allowed to collapse. However, Goldman Sachs was not hit as hard during the financial crisis because their risk exposure to the toxic securitised products created out of bad debts was significantly lower. Goldman Sachs have received much criticism for their business conduct but in relation to their decision-making on risk assessment they did comparatively well. Why? They came through the GFC stronger than their competitors due to one meeting on 14 December 2006. Goldman's Chief Financial Officer, David Viniar, and Chief Risk Officer, Craig Brederick met with thirteen senior colleagues to review the volatility of the subprime mortgage market and ten days of losses of their mortgage-related products. According to an interview by Joe Nocera with David Viniar, the group examined their VaR numbers and their other risk models and they talked about how the mortgage-backed securities market felt. Nocera quotes Viniar as saying: 'Our guys said that it felt like it was going to get worse before it got better. So we made a decision: let's get closer to home.'[4] Notice the word 'felt'. Fifteen senior executives at Goldman Sachs made a decision ultimately on what they 'felt'. In other words, they deployed their intuition. Sure they checked the numbers, but other firms were looking at similar numbers and feeling secure in the predictability of their risk management models. Not so, Goldman. According to the US Financial Crisis Inquiry Commission, Goldman reduced its own mortgage risk following this meeting through to August 2007 by creating and selling approximately US\$25.4 billion of

CDOs.[5] CDOs are asset-based securities split into different risk classes and Goldman was able to 'unload its own inventory of other CDO securities and mortgage-backed securities.' The Goldman sales team were instructed to even sell at a loss following the December meeting. By significantly reducing its subprime securities, Goldman was able to secure itself against the financial tsunami that was to sweep Wall Street during the last quarter of 2008.

Despite the ever-increasing size of the knowledge databases available to organisations to make the most informed decisions, the risk for making bad decisions remains. Goldman's willingness to take a major decision that could not be fully supported by the facts at the time proved to be the right call. We make no comment on the methods that they involved to unbundle their risk. We simply record that quality decisions usually require facts plus another quality that we refer to as intuition. Deploying intuition, we believe is a vital factor in making quality decisions.

Intuition first

We sometimes see intuition at work in expressions of insight. When we express these insights we are expressing a hypothesis which will then direct us towards the appropriate facts to validate it. Great innovations and ideas begin with an insight. Facts are interesting but often useless without intuitive insights. As Peter Drucker once said, in making an effective decision one does not start with the facts: 'There are no facts unless one has a criterion of relevance.'[6] Intuitive insight (sometimes expressed as an opinion) is the criterion of relevance.

Intuitive insight is a 'sight from within' that describes the ability observable in entrepreneurs who can see or sense ahead the opportunities and risks not observable through normal working with data analytics. Su Xin, founder of the Chinese Go-High fund, began his entrepreneurship aged 40 by buying a commercial portion of the Kaide Huaxi buildings in Shanghai in 2009. Su Xin's insight was that commercial real estate was undervalued. Then he looked for the facts which supported his insight. Before building a business model, Su Xin made the Kaide Huaxi investment as 'a random choice:' 'It's totally unlike what they tell you in the textbooks, which is: first, find a direction; then decide what resources are needed. Reality isn't as perfect as a textbook.'[7] By 2012, Go-High was named among the Top 10 RMB-denominated private real estate funds by CBN Magazine. Su Xin had left a safe and lucrative job as a board director of SOHO China, a prime office space developer which he describes as 'a decision I made with my heart.'

When it comes to making a decision our Monk needs to be nurtured to release insights to balance the rational data that our Suit is keen to process. The diagram overleaf illustrates the alignment that we need between insights and facts.

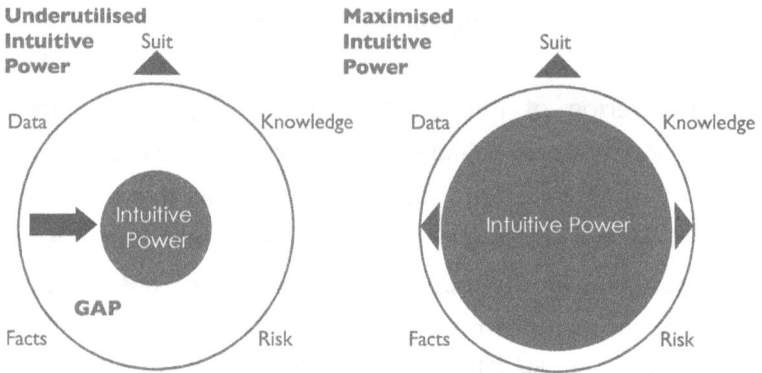

If Monk and Suit are not aligned then data, facts and knowledge do not interact with the Monk and intuitive insight is not 'activated'. If Monk and Suit are aligned then intuitive insight interacts with data and adds a further dimension to decision-making.

In recent years, we have come to understand that the best decisions we have made in life and work have been as a result of following our hearts. By that we mean that we have not rushed towards a logical set of career objectives, weighed up financial pros and cons and planned our path. Rather, we have felt our way forward, giving time to reflect and sense what is happening in our environment, what draws us forward and what doesn't. Rational processing should follow as a second-order process when life changes present themselves: mind should follow heart and not the other way around.

Sometimes our intuitive instincts surprise us. Perhaps we have observed an opportunity at a subconscious level which is then 'presented' to us consciously as if out of the blue. Mike remembers, for example, that during a flight from Shanghai to London in October 2008, he experienced a powerful inner sense, a vision (perhaps a call) that he should move to Shanghai. Yet no one had invited him! Although he was surprised by the strong sense that this was a next life step for him, he did not feel shaken by the prospect. Shanghai was not in his mind or plan at all, but he chose not to close down the impression he had received, but rather to explore it, discuss it with family and friends, and weigh it. The Shanghai plan for Mike emerged as he kept his inner eyes open to the events and the opportunities that opened up for him over the following four months before he made the final decision to move. Mike had known and responded to such intuitions before and, in each case, there were plenty of rational reasons not to respond to them - mainly the risk of getting it wrong and facing the loss of security (and maybe status) of his circumstances at the time.

You may think that this sounds risky as you can't trust what you may feel in your heart. You may be afraid that you could make a foolish choice or one that leads to a big mistake. You have to step out of your rational comfort zone and step out in trust. True intuition will not ultimately lead you to failure even though you may find moments of regret about certain decisions you took that did not appear to work out at the time. It is sometimes difficult to discern the difference between the activity and thoughts of the mind and the impulses that arise from true intuition.

True intuition will guide you through life's journey well even though you may sometimes have to go through tough times. Developing a sensitivity to your intuition takes time and practice as we shall see from the stories in this chapter.

Sometimes we need to take a step back from the 'facts' and the normative and logical mental responses to the 'facts' and ask: 'What do I feel is really happening behind the data and the facts?' Pause, take some breaths and tease out your gut feeling. For example, for the next three decisions when you have to make a rational decision, take a five-minute break, and use that time to listen to your emotions, gut feelings and body. How are they responding to the decision that you are making? Does it feel like it's the right way forward? If not, is there anything you need to change in making your decision? Your intuition is partly informed by previous experiences and you may find a caution or a positive feeling towards an opportunity that comes your way. When the decision to be made is a shared decision, encourage your colleagues to explore their feelings to the facts as well as the logical options that are presented. In a meeting and before making a decision, you could share some questions such as:

What do I feel?
What does my gut tell me?
Is this the right thing to do?
Are there some hesitations that we feel that need to be aired?

Entrepreneurs trust their intuition

The idea of entrepreneurs trusting their intuition and following their heart is not new. John Mackey, the co-founder of Whole Foods Market, a US$12 billion food retailing business borrowed US$45,000 in 1978 to start his first store in Austin, Texas. In his book with Raj Sisodia entitled *Conscious Capitalism* Mackey writes about business as a 'wonderful vehicle for both personal and organizational learning and growth.' Mackey recounts what he calls 'awakenings' of rising consciousness in his life and work and recalls that in this early twenties 'I made what has proven to be a wise decision: a lifelong commitment to follow my heart wherever this would lead me – which has been on a wonderful journey of adventure, purpose, growth, and love.'[8]

At business schools in East and West students are seeking to make a career switch by completing a world-class MBA program. Career-switching is not necessary if you have already found fulfilment in a particular career path. In a fast-changing business world, leading companies have the HR flexibility to enable job changes to take place. Companies led by entrepreneurs are good at spotting a talented and truly committed person with the potential to take on a new challenge outside their experience.

Richard Branson, the entrepreneur behind the vast group of Virgin enterprises, has always tried to get people to reinvent themselves. When Richard needed to overhaul Virgin Retail in 1988 he appointed Simon Burke to be CEO. Simon Burke was a development manager in the Virgin Group and in Branson's words had 'no obvious qualifications to turn a large chain of unsuccessful record shops into a chain of successful ones.' But despite this, Branson was able to say: 'I was certain that, if anyone could do it, he could.'[9] Simon restructured the business and by June 1989, Virgin Retail produced its first ever profit. Both men had taken a risk, Simon by putting himself forward and Richard by appointing him.

To follow your gut instinct takes courage - the courage to take the risks and the potential consequence of failure. The idea of a Virgin Megastore in the Champs Elysées in Paris was high risk and there were many well-founded arguments why the Board 'hated the idea.' But Richard Branson was inspired by the idea and in a typical move of unorthodoxy, announced in a television commercial, standing on the Champs Elyées, that the next Virgin Megastore was going to be right there - in spite of the fact that he knew the entire board was against the idea. The conviction came from within, a mix of insight, intuition, experience and a capacity to see a business opportunity not visible through normal business processes. The Paris Megastore was 'an incredible success' smashing all sales forecasts.[10]

Leaders who follow their gut instinct can save a company a lot of time and money. British entrepreneur,

Alan Sugar, handed over control of the Amstrad Group to a new board when it became a listed company. The new CEO, David Rogers, wanted to introduce inkjet printing into Amstrad. In 1993, based on work conducted by a management consultancy and support from the Board, Rogers recommended the acquisition of a Swedish inkjet manufacturer and asked Alan Sugar for his view:

> I told him if he was asking me to make the decision, the answer was no. It was a wise decision. Eventually, the Swedish company went into liquidation and no one bought the technology, which turned out to be total garbage compared to that being developed by Hewlett-Packard and other Japanese companies.[11]

Earlier in the professional evaluation of the target company Lord Sugar had been excluded for fear of biasing the rational process of due diligence. At the outset, Sugar assessed the Swedish business and believed its operation and products had no long-term viability. Sugar's reference here to a 'wise decision' is the ability to combine intuitive insight with fact-based thinking in making a decision. The facts that had been collated and reviewed by the consultants and by Rogers pointed to making the acquisition. But Sugar's more intuitive judgment of the facts and perhaps the way he viewed the world from his experience led him to conclude differently. Balancing a rational approach with intuitive insight is wise decision-making in a business context and is an important principle in the life of a Suited Monk. The Wisdom of a Suited Monk is the subject of chapter ten.

Following your heart or your gut instinct begins by first cultivating and testing new ideas on a smaller scale before carefully trying it out when there is no data or future. How about launching a new Greek yoghurt in the US when you are told that Americans would not eat yoghurt unless it's sweet and coloured? This is what Hamdi Ulukaya did in 2005 in response to what he called the 'colourful sugar-mixed cups' that passed for yoghurt in the US. Ulukaya decided that he would make and sell the plain yoghurt he had grown up with in eastern Turkey. Ulukaya's story was told in the Financial Times in May 2013 under the title: 'Founder follows his gut instincts',[12] followed by a further story one month later announcing the news that he had been named Ernst & Young World Entrepreneur of the Year.[13] The theme of these stories was that Ulukaya had founded a new Greek yoghurt brand called Chobani after buying a redundant Kraft yoghurt factory with a US$1 million grant from the Small Business Administration, a US federal agency. His lawyer said he was nuts and with Greek yoghurt only accounting for one per cent of the US yoghurt market in 2007, it was likely that market research and strategy advice would have concurred. But Ulukaya did not listen: he re-outfitted the factory with custom straining machines that could mass-produce authentic Greek yoghurt. Ulukaya did not begin with the facts of market research he began with an insight:

> We always trusted in our instincts and the messages that were coming directly from the consumers. We've never done studies. We've never done market research. That's what I believe in as an entrepreneur. You need to see not the small tree over the ground, but you have to see the seed underneath. We have to see things before anybody else has seen it yet.[14]

From a knowledge-based perspective, the notion of seeing things before anybody else has seen them is not an acceptable basis to proceed: it is not 'fact-based thinking' and not the way of thinking that VPs have been schooled to manage their organisations. But Ulukaya's intuition and foresight have been vindicated by the subsequent business facts: 'His concept proved a supermarket sensation', according to marketing pundits.[15] In six years, the Chobani brand is now half of the US Greek yoghurt market, with over $1bn in annual sales. In 2013, the size of the Greek yoghurt share of market had risen to 35 per cent. Chobani has been responsible for growing a new healthy yoghurt market category in the US.

Intuition in due diligence

Peter Buytaert, who we introduced in chapter two, has found the need to exercise intuition alongside fact-finding and rational skills in his investment consulting work. This combination is vital when conducting due diligence on a company target for acquisition. One of Peter's Private Equity clients was considering the acquisition of a privately held company in Malaysia. The due diligence team was composed of Peter, a legal counsel, a team from one of the big five auditing firms and a VP from HQ. The team did not find any major potential 'red flags' and from a rational and data perspective, the company passed the due diligence tests.

But Peter intuitively felt that the data room was not revealing the full picture: 'It is a case where you follow the book on due diligence and tick all the boxes but when wisdom kicks in, the mix of technical competencies and leadership experience builds a new dimension which makes one plus one equal to three.' Peter focused on getting to know the CFO and invited him to dinner and showed interest in understanding him personally better, including his family. 'Even when I did manage to build trust with the CFO, it still required a lot of 'reading between the lines' and following 'gut feel' to ask the right questions and extract the real answers and to better understand the underlying current and politics in the organisation which included a chairman who was invisible in the process. Following the book was not enough. It required what some would judge to be a 'waste of time' to have conversations unrelated to the deal to reveal the truth of the deal evaluation.'

The day after Peter's dinner conversation the CFO

called Peter to his office and said that he had placed additional boxes of information to the data room not previously included in the document list. The additional documents revealed fundamental problems: the company's shares were actually held by the bank and not by the 'owners' who tried to sell a significantly different picture of the financial health of the organisation. The team called off the acquisition. Without Peter's intuitive insight and cross-cultural experience about organisational behaviours, the expert team would have arrived at the wrong investment decision if they had confined their review to the data room.

Nurturing the intuitive instinct

If our Monk and Suit work together very effectively, the intuitive sense will be nurtured through the daily events of life which validate that we are on the right path. Often it can be the many 'coincidental' meetings with people which seem to form part of our journey.

Sometimes we meet people by accident, but it's rarely an accident or coincidence. Ideas or insight from the Monk that pop up are the seeds that are planted within you. Those seeds need to grow. Raf's deep sense that he should go to Shanghai in 2008 didn't make sense to him at that time, but it was a seed that led to him meeting Mike and working with GLO. He sees all the people in his path have come to him for a reason. The insight to make the move to

Shanghai was more than just for a job.

Think about a time in your life when you received a new job opportunity. How did it come about? How did you meet your future boss or life partner? Was it by accident or because of an unexpected decision to make a change? Often when you make an unexpected decision, you feel that you just have to and you go for it. And generally the right things happen – we're not talking about impulsive stock market investments here!

So when making decisions, life's elements often work synchronously. Steve Jobs once said:

> You can't connect the dots looking forward; you can only connect them looking backwards. So you have to trust that the dots will somehow connect in your future. You have to trust in something - your gut, destiny, life, karma, whatever. This approach has never let me down, and it has made all the difference in my life. [16]

Your intuitive self is a gift which should be honoured and nurtured. In difficult times or difficult decisions your Monk will guide you. This is what we refer to in the next chapter as the Flow. If you are not sure, exercise trust in your intuition. Often the best decisions are made 'without thinking' but when responding sponta-neously to life situations.

Reflective 'on the job' questions

1. How much intuition did I use today during decision making?
2. Do I trust myself even though rationally it is not certain what is going to happen?
3. How much does my team use intuition in decision making?

1. This quotation has been attributed to Albert Einstein who made similar comments but there is no evidence recorded that these were his words.

2. Source: www.nytimes.com/2009/01/04/magazine/04risk-thtml?pagewanted=all

3. Source: www.salon.com/2013/01/06/help_us_nate_silver/?utsource=scribol.com&utm_medium=referral&utm_campaign=scribol.com

4. Joe Nocera, 2009, "Risk Mismanagement", New York Times, 2 January, Source: www.nytimes.com/2009/01/04/magazine/04risk-t.html?pagewanted=all

5. Financial Crisis Inquiry Commission, 2011, "The Financial Crisis Inquiry Report: The Final Report of the National Commission on the Causes of the Financial and Economic Crisis in the United States, Including Dissenting Views", *Cosimo Reports*, New York, NY, p.236.

6. Drucker, P. F., 1974, *Management: Tasks, Responsibilities, Practices*, Harper & Row, New York, NY, p.471.

7. Su Xin interviewed by Kelly Chen and Shawn Shen in *The Link, CEIBS Alumni Magazine*, CEIBS, Shanghai, vol 2., 2013, p. 35.

8. Mackey, J and Sisodia, R., 2013, *Conscious Capitalism*, Harvard Business Review Press, Boston, MA, p.7.

9. Branson, R., 1998, *Losing My Virginity*, Virgin Publishing, London, p.259.

10. *ibid*, p.258.

11. Sugar, A., 2010, *What You See Is What You Get*, Macmillan, Basingstoke, p.366.

12. Fifield, A., 2013, "Founder follows his gut instincts", *Financial Times*, 9 April.

13. Moule, J., 2013, "Victory for the American dream", *Financial Times*, 11 June.

14. Hamdi Ulukaya quoted by Fifield, A., 2013 op.cit.

15. Urbanski, A., 2013, "Chobani Challenges Consumers to Get Real", 6 March, *dmnews.com* and Watson, E., 2013, "The rise and rise of Greek yoghurt. But is the rise sustainable?", 9 April. Source: Foodnavigator-usa.com.

16. Steve Jobs speaking at the Commencement address at Stanford Graduate School of Business, 12 June, 2005. Source: http://news.stanford.edu/news/2005/june15/jobs-061505.html

5. TRUST THE FLOW

All my professional life I have been going in directions which others thought were foolish, and about which I have had many doubts myself. But I have never regretted moving in directions which "felt right", even though I have often felt lonely or foolish at the time. I have found that when I have trusted some inner non-intellectual sensing, I have discovered wisdom in the move.

Carl Rogers (psychiatrist)[1]

Carl Rogers was one of the most influential psychologists in American history and wrote about his 'total organismic sensing of a situation' being more trustworthy than his intellect. In the quote above he speaks about 'non-intellectual sensing' and right upfront we need to give a scientific health warning: THIS CHAPTER HAS NO SCIENTIFIC BASIS.[2]

Now we have said that, we can explore experiences in life that cannot be verified by science, or, what Immanuel

Kant called experiences governed by the 'transcendental aesthetic'[3]. A materialist belief-system relies on the central assumption that everything is essentially material or physical (logical knowledge). Sensory perception is not to be trusted and can be illusory. But as Rupert Sheldrake, a cell biologist and parapsychologist, has pointed out, leading journals such as Behavioural and Brain Sciences and the Journal of Consciousness Studies publish many articles that reveal deep problems with the materialism doctrine.[4] Many scientists have acknowledged the reality of human sensory perception even though it cannot be adequately explained.[5]

We respect a rational approach to life but we also respect the view that there are phenomena of consciousness that cannot be fully explained by science or neuroscience in particular. A chapter that acknowledges the existence of Flow takes us into the realm of metaphysics and spirituality which psychologists and neuroscientists are still exploring. Mihály Csíkszentmihályi first used the term 'Flow' to describe the positive feelings of being fully immersed, energised, and aligned with the task at hand.[6]

You can visualise Flow as a river of passion and purpose within. As our friend and trainer Larry Lee says: 'Flowing with the river is simply following your intuition, passion, dream and purpose. It is a journey full of risks, uncertainty and challenges but also with meaning, peace and happiness.'

Each of us has a set of talents to take us towards

a fulfilling life journey. We each have our own 'river of life'. This river provides the energy to take us forward in our 'spiritual kayak' although it feels risky and it may not appear to be the most direct route to take us to where we think we should like to go. If you have tried steering a kayak through a fast moving river, you will know that going with the flow of the river can be hard work at times. It is not a smooth or easy ride but it's your river and all your senses will come to the fore in steering your way to the unique opportunities that life will bring to you. You will be surprised as you too discover your latent talents 'kicking in'.

Hiking your way through the mountains rather than going with the river enables you to control your journey and appears to be the more rational route but it can heighten the Gap between your Suit and your Monk and you could miss the unexpected opportunities that life brings you in the river.

We also understand Flow as a level of connectedness with others, one which can even involve the experience of a shared consciousness and connectedness to others – 'ultimate empathy'. William Hutchinson Murray paints a picture of the Flow of life in words that are usually attributed to Goethe:

> *Until one is committed, there is hesitancy, the chance to draw back. Concerning all acts of initiative (and creation), there is one elementary truth, the ignorance of*

which kills countless ideas and splendid plans: that the moment one definitely commits oneself, then Providence moves too. All sorts of things occur to help one that would never otherwise have occurred. A whole stream of events issues from the decision, raising in one's favour all manner of unforeseen incidents and meetings and material assistance, which no man could have dreamed would have come his way. Whatever you can do, or dream you can do, begin it. Boldness has genius, power, and magic in it. Begin it now.[7]

Flow is 'Providence' and 'magic' along our life journey, although both terms are unscientific and rely on a subjective interpretation of phenomena.

Connecting to the Flow

Quantum physics tells us that everything, including light, is made of minute moving particles and everything is part of a sea of energy: nothing is solid, including our bodies. Some people, such as Reiki practitioners, claim to see an electromagnetic field or particles of energy in colours around the human body which they call the 'aura'. Neuroscientists, biologists and cognitive scientists use the language of consciousness rather than the language of energy or spirit. You can't see consciousness but it is the 'stuff' of our existence. Perhaps this is why neuroscientists still struggle to demonstrate that consciousness is entirely explained by brain activity. Prof Alva Noë's work in perception and consciousness theory at the University of California supports a growing view that consciousness is not to be found in the brain as a kind of 'mind-body':

> *Human experience is a dance that unfolds in the world and with others. You are not your brain. We are not locked up in a prison of our own ideas and sensations. The phenomenon of consciousness, like that of life itself, is a world-involving dynamic process.*[8]

Raymond Tallis is a neuroscientist and an eminent professor in clinical neuroscience research. He argues:

> *Our consciousness, and the engines that shape it, cannot be found solely in the stand-alone brain; or even just in a brain in a body; or even in a brain interacting with other brains in bodies. It participates in, and is part of, a community of minds built up by conscious human beings over hundreds of thousands of years.*[9]

This idea of connectedness to each other in a community of minds is not a new idea. The great philosopher Immanuel Kant wrote of the 'transcendental aesthetic'[10], sociologist Peter Berger[11] wrote about 'signals of transcendence' and Luk Bouckaert, an emeritus professor at Leuven, writes of spirituality as a reconnection to the inner self and 'a search for universal values that lift the individual above his egocentric strivings, a deep empathy with all living beings and the desire to keep in touch with the Source of life (whatever name we give it).'[12] Connecting to your deepest self is a spiritual connection. Our Monk has a perceptivity that goes beyond the mind and body into what might be called a spiritual level of perception. Living with heightened awareness of yourself and the world is extremely powerful. With a more finely tuned level of clarity, you can 'see' ahead and know how to respond to the challenges and opportunities that present themselves in life and work. You too, like Dr Rogers, can move in directions that 'felt right'. Making this happen from your internal world takes courage. You must believe in and trust yourself; surrender and follow your intuition and inner journey; accept things as they are and be willing to let go of old thoughts, beliefs, negative emotions and attachments that are no longer useful along your journey. Initially you may experience temporary discomfort and unease. Maybe you'll find that unsettling emotions and challenges from past experiences come to the surface. But the more you become aware of your inner being, the clearer and easier your life and career path will become.

You can compare this journey to a well with a special water pump that only works in one direction. Once it's been opened, it can't be closed again. The further you raise the handle, the more water will Flow out. Similarly, once your journey has begun, the process is naturally revealed. All you need to do is follow the Flow; it isn't necessary to know where it will end.

When you make decisions related to career development it's important that you are able to identify when it's time to move on and time to grow to the next level. This growth will be determined by your level of awareness and being. Somehow you can feel it - it's a 'knowing'. Following the Flow can be challenging, especially when it appears it isn't Flowing. Not knowing where the Flow will take you can be challenging too, especially in a business context. You may have to face up to the worst of your fears about what could go wrong or that you risk making the wrong decision. When there does not appear to be Flow happening, it is tempting to make things happen. You may well make things happen, but waiting and pausing for life to bring you the next step can often take you into new paths that your mind could never have designed for you. This does not mean that you are inactive in working towards the next phase, rather you seek to work with the different waves in your world and allow your vision to be shifted. This requires an inner poise which comes the more you trust your monk to perceive and see new paths ahead. Allow your monk to observe your mind and your ego.

Flow to navigate the VUCA World

The VUCA world is the external world we face now with its Volatility, Uncertainty, Complexity and Ambiguity. Moving with the Flow of life, being ready to enter unfamiliar territory, taking calculated risks keeps us resilient against the impacts of the VUCA world. We could get stressed and burned out by the sheer level of insecurity that the VUCA world threatens, but maintaining a healthy and happy Monk and living under the law of acceptance helps us to cope with the losses and challenges that come. One basic truth is that all the complexity and insecurity makes life in the VUCA world especially difficult. Psychiatrist, M. Scott Peck, says that once we truly understand and accept this truth then life is no longer difficult because we transcend the difficulties.[13]

Living in the Flow of life is essentially living under the innate wisdom of your Monk, the indefinable spirit that gives you a higher level of consciousness than just your brainpower. Living in the Flow of your Monk provides you with emotional regulation and the ability to detach from a purely self-interested focus and actually enhances your ability to deal with the VUCA world. A good example of this is found in the work of Dr Thomas C. Redman. In a Harvard Business Review blog, Redman summarised his findings about the advantages to companies of being 'data driven': better quality decisions and greater profitability.[14] Leaving aside methodological questions about how you define and measure 'data driven' behaviour as a factor of company profitability, the basic idea is interesting. In a business world where Big Data is king, asking the question, 'Are you data driven?', seems to be the 'on message' question in the VUCA world. Redman spells this message out with twelve 'Traits of the Data-Driven' and invites his blog readers to score themselves against the list. He says that the data-driven:

1. Make decisions at the lowest possible level.
2. Bring as much diverse data to any situation as they possibly can.
3 Use data to develop a deeper understanding of their worlds.
4. Develop an appreciation for variation.
5. Deal reasonably well with uncertainty.
6. Integrate their ability to understand data and its implications and their intuitions.
7. Recognise the importance of high-quality data and invest to improve.
8. Are good experimenters and researchers.
9. Recognise that decision criteria can vary with circumstances.
10. Recognise that making a decision is only step one.
11. Work hard to learn new skills and bring new data and new data technologies (big data, predictive analytics, metadata management, etc) into their organisations.
12. Learn from their mistakes.

What intrigues us from this list is how many of the traits are not drawn from what we may call the rational cognitive realm of the mind. At least half the traits are more in keeping with the intuitive and reflective traits of the Monk. For example, learning from mistakes requires self awareness and the ability observe oneself in the situations of life. Dealing well with uncertainty is essentially following the Flow, regarded by wisdom psychologists as a component of wisdom, a human capacity nurtured by our Monk which we shall discuss in chapter ten.

The VaR model that we referred to in chapter four utilises millions of data points to assess the riskiness of a portfolio investment. But investment traders relied upon VaR too readily, focusing on the risk numbers generated by VaR and the immediate temptations of large personal benefits. Data needs to be understood, challenged and interpreted. Redman's 'data driven' title is as much about wise reflection on the data and he includes intuition amongst the traits of understanding data. The Goldman Sachs team that we referred to in chapter four provides a good example of the way in which intuition or 'feeling' can be acknowledged in a data-driven environment. The GS team went with the Flow and began to offload mortgage backed securities.

Tara Posely trusts the Flow

Tara Poseley began her career with Gap Inc and took the opportunity to create a range of activewear for women. The standard way of presenting the business case to the senior management committee was through a formal slide presentation. It was Tara's first ever formal presentation but after a few minutes she felt it wasn't going well. She decided to stop the presentation, abandon the slides she had prepared, and simply follow her intuition - a bold move in front of the board of the company. What followed would change the way Gap Inc approaches Women's Activewear. A new Flow started to come from within her and she began her presentation simply to turn to a rack of prototype garments behind her and began handing them out whilst speaking to the CEO and other senior officers. After the presentation, Tara was given the green light, and GapBody Women's Activewear was launched.

It takes courage to follow your intuition and accept moments like this because we tend to be risk averse and do not easily give way to intuitive instincts. It is as though our rational mind quickly provides good, reasoned arguments why we should not follow intuitive insights which can be easily dismissed as being irrational. Tara Poseley later explained her experience in a rather unusual way:

> Yes, you have to have the vision. And you have to have the deep intention that goes with it. But you also have to have the incredible capacity for self-observation and course correction in real time. The universe wants to help. But you must be able to observe and listen.[15]

Unlikely words to come from a person who became Chief

Product Officer at lululemon athletica in 2013.

Our mental processes most associated with the Suit that we wear for the 'external world' would rather that we choose different explanations for our decision-making. So an explanation which would satisfy the Suit might sound like this: 'Following a 12 month study of consumer data in the US apparel market, noting the sales trend of niche activewear brands, having conducted extensive qualitative and quantitative consumer testing, we present this 200 page business plan to demonstrate the potential for a trial launch.' All such facts are eminently important but Tara Poseley was courageous enough to make a 'course correction', accept that the current reality was not working and followed a Flow of energy from within rather than the security of her prepared presentation.

From the Gap perspective, Tara followed the Flow and as a result enlarged her Monk, decreasing the Gap which enabled her to overcome fear with courage, and sense intuitively what would convince the Board.

We experience Flow when we allow our lives to unfold moment by moment overcoming the need to continually drive ourselves towards goals that are resistant to our efforts. This Flow is a constant surrendering and trusting to what life brings to us in life and career opportunities: we follow our intuition and allow events to happen and then Flow with them observing and acting appropriately as we go. Yes, there are likely to be some failures and errors along the way, but more often than not we believe that following your heart will lead to the best outcomes. The questions from our minds can often be answered by facts, but the deeper questions from our hearts are better addressed through a strong sense of self awareness and aligning our gifts and purpose to the opportunities that our life journey presents to us. This is Flow and this is the work of our Monk.

How can we Flow in life?

We inhabit two worlds: the external world and the internal world. The external world is continually changing and is largely out of our control although we may try hard to control it. It is the world we view through our eyes and beyond our self and the world in which we project our image. Our true self is what we have been referring to as our inner Monk.

Your Monk represents a reflective, self-observant and spiritual mode of being – your Monk is always with you whereas the 'you' that experiences the external world is changeable. Your job role might change, your relationships might change, your community and social culture might change. Whatever you experience in the external world is liable to change. You may experience happiness but it could quickly be replaced by depression because you are allowing your external world to influence your inner life. But your Monk can experience a deep and lasting joy and purpose whatever is happening in the external world because your

Monk is the core of your internal world – the place from which insight, creativity and true joy are created. Your Monk is sensitised to the Flows of life and movements in the environment that we feel at a subconscious level.

How can we be more in tune with our Monk, our true self? We believe that the more that we tune in to our Monk, the more our journey in the external world can be fulfilling and purposeful. Allowing your Monk to guide you involves the challenging process of letting go of the things that the external world tells you are most important: where you were educated, your social status, your financial status and the 'badges' of your position in society. Letting go is a matter of the heart and cannot be dealt with as a mental transaction. It is a profound acceptance of all that life brings to you – including suffering. It is an acceptance that life is difficult and sometimes painful and that you cannot hedge yourself from the risks of living.

Your Monk is well-equipped to help you cope with pain and suffering and to help you overcome the restrictions created by others and yourself about what you can accomplish in your life journey. If you allow, your Monk can take you outside the objections of your mind and help you temporarily to suspend your judgement about why something may or may not work out. Your Monk will sense the Flow and the energies of your world. All you need to do is trust this inner voice or instinct. Sometimes this will be easy and sometimes it will be hard.

When challenges come, the best way to respond is

not through emotional outbursts such as anger or panic, but rather by accepting, perhaps even surrendering, to what seems to be happening to you in the external VUCA world. Then you step back to the Monk within and observe the challenge from a different viewpoint. Sometimes your Monk needs time to observe and process, sometimes your Monk will instantaneously provide you with a flash of inspiration about how to respond to the challenge. Your mental and rational processes can then follow on from that inspiration to check the options and the best way to carry out your inspiration.

Simply being able to distinguish the role of your Monk from the role of the mind in facing challenges can be the key to living a happy and purposeful life. Living in the Flow of our purpose requires a discipline of our mental and egotistical processes. The idea of us having a Suit that we 'wear' over our Monk is to distinguish the two modes of our experience of life.

There is no reason why we cannot be fully true to our inner Monk (the real us) when we wear our Suit. Being yourself in your Suit means a full acceptance of yourself for who you really are (strengths and weaknesses) so that you can go out towards others without the need to manipulate others for your own ends. Essentially this means loving yourself first so that you can go out towards other people in honesty and openness even though you are aware of the risks of rejection.

Flowing with Acceptance

In chapter three we discussed the laws of rejection and acceptance and these laws are very important in trusting the Flow from within. The external world brings us the experience of rejection, while the internal world generates acceptance. This is because our Suit may reject a new reality or changes that do not match our expectations. As a result stress increases unless we are able to manage stress from our Monk. How do I react when waiting to meet a business partner for an important dinner and they have not turned up? There is no message and there is no reply to my calls: an expectation is dashed. Stress is the result, not only of such dashed expectations, but the response we have towards those expectations and events. One of the causes of stress is an egoic rejection of the uncomfortable realities that face us and the expression of our rejection can be anger or bitterness, or both.

Our Monk has the capacity to observe circumstances in a detached way so that we can observe the potential for the frustration and anger of a situation and prepare ourselves for it. The reality of the circumstance may be difficult to change, but by becoming an observer of the circumstance – and even of our own reaction to it – we can reduce stress.

Acceptance can be very difficult because we think that if we accept a situation or something about ourselves, we shall lose our sense of control. We think that we shall become somehow less because we don't defend ourselves. But practising acceptance is actually a source of inner strength. Accepting what is happening to you doesn't mean you should have less self-esteem or that you should let someone else take advantage of you. Acceptance means that you allow the external event to happen without attaching your ego to the results of the event. Maybe there was a time that you expected to receive an invitation to a social event but never received the invitation. Maybe you expected a promotion but someone else got it. These are events that can easily cause hurt. If so, then it is your Suit that feels the hurt. Your Monk is unaffected because s/he does not rely on social cues to live happily or purposefully.

In our experience learning to respond to challenges to the ego from the Monk within becomes easier with practice. Whenever you accept your current situation, or what is happening around you, you move closer to the true feelings of your Monk. Accepting your current situation allows you to respond to it more peacefully and to clarify your thinking on how best to embark on the next steps without the interference of negative emotions. As Joseph Campbell said, 'We must be willing to get rid of the life we've planned, so as to have the life that is waiting for us.'[16]

One man who participated in a workshop led by Raf very much wanted to join the US Army as a combat medic. But the maximum enlistment age had recently dropped from 42 to 35 and although he intended to apply for an age waiver, he thought he would most likely be denied because he was 41. He told Raf: 'It will be a disappointment if I am denied because of my age but I can accept it and continue with my life knowing the universe has a plan for me. Being receptive, I know good things will come. Had I not taken your course, this would have been a major setback for me but after your weekend workshop, I can accept it and look to the good things in my life.'

Acceptance can be difficult to practise at first because it requires letting go of the fear of the unknown, the fear of change and the fear of losing ourselves. We feel discomfort because our ego feels secure with the status quo and must adjust to fit the changes we're experiencing on our life journey. The more you practise acceptance, the easier it is to allow things to come to you and to embrace them, rather than reject them.

And don't allow disappointment or even despair to result from expectations being unrealised: observe your expectations rather than being attached to them. You can be attached to expectations or observe expectations. If you operate purely from the mind and ego (attachment) you are more likely to suffer stress. If you operate from your Monk, you allow the external event to be disregarded without the feelings of suffering or stress. Aim to be the observer of your mind and ego; if you take the role as an observer in a crisis situation you can make better decisions.

In 2012 the first Wise Management Conference in China was held at the China Europe International

Business School in Shanghai. Sixty delegates from around the world came together to present their papers on Wisdom. Two of the keynote speakers for the event were coming from Australia to deliver their presentations. However at Sydney airport they were refused boarding as they had not realised that they required a visa to enter China. We had to set up a video link for them to give their keynote speeches at the conference the next day.

We are confronted with sudden, unexpected and unwanted circumstances in the course of our daily work. Our Suit is challenged by situations that are not what we had planned or expected and our Monk has to deal with the situation from within and we have to adjust ourselves with the Flow.

In essence, we believe that living as a Suited Monk means that we can tap into a source of energy that guides us. At times we might even feel that this energy comes to us from outside us. Whatever we may feel the source is, this is the energy of life and it is our individual life. Check out your sensitivity to the Flow by reflecting on the questions in the box overleaf.

Reflective Exercises

When difficulties occur, are you able to trust yourself that everything will work out well in the end?

Are you able to surrender in difficult times in your life and work and act as Tara Poseley did when she found herself in a difficult situation?

Think of an action that you took recently that did not work out too well. If it was a failure, call it a failure. Only your Suit might feel offended by that conclusion. Did you truly feel that the action was heading in the right direction? If so, stay true to your vision, but not under pressures from the external world. Rather, allow the Flow of energy to come from within. If you reflect that the direction was wrong, then just put it down to experience and do not allow your mind or the external world tell you that you are a failure. Actually failure or worrying or putting ourselves down about past decisions doesn't exist. All experiences are learning and self-awareness opportunities to help us grow and mature to the next level in our lives.

1 Rogers, C., 1961, *On Becoming a Person,* Houghton Mifflin, Boston, MA, p.22.

2. We are in sympathy with philosopher Mary Midgley's argument in *Are You an Illusion?* (Acumen, 2014) in which she opposes a scientific arrogance that seeks to "reduce our direct, everyday experience of reality to terms of something more distant, preferably involving statistics and (where possible) machinery".

3. Kant, I., 1781/2008, *Kant's Critiques,* Wilder Publications, Radford, WA, p.37.

4. Sheldrake, R., 2012, *The Science Delusion,* Coronet, London, p. 10.

5. See, for example, the works of biologist Rupert Sheldrake. Karl Popper in his *Logik Der Forschung* claimed that 'the empirical basis of natural science has nothing 'absolute' about it. Science does not rest upon a solid bedrock.' (p.111).

6. Csíkszentmihályi, M., 1990, Flow: *The Psychology of Optimal Experience,* Harper-Row, New York.

7. William Hutchinson Murray, 1951, *The Scottish Himalayan Expedition.*

8. Noë, A., 2009, *Out of Our Heads: Why You are Not Your Brain and Other Lessons from the Biology of Consciousness,* Hill and Wang, New York, p. xiii.

9. Tallis, R, 2011, Tallis, R., Aping *Mankind: Neuromania, Darwinitis and the Misrepresentation of Humanity,* Acumen Publishing, Durham, p.11.

10. Immanuel Kant refers to sensation as meaning that is derived from the senses and which contributes to cognition - our mental processes – our faculty of knowing. (*Critique of Pure Reason, 1781* in *Kant's Critiques,* 2008, Wilder Publications, Radford, WA).

11. Berger, P., 1969, *A Rumor of Angels: Modern Society and the Rediscovery of the Supernatural,* Doubleday Anchor, New York, NY.

12. Bouckaert, L., 2007, "Spirituality in Economics", ed. Bouckaert, L and Zsolnai, L., *Spirituality as a Public Good,* Garant, Antwerp, p. 13.

13. Peck, M. S., 1978, *The Road Less Travelled,* Arrow Books, London, p.13.

14. Redman, T. C., 2013, "Are you data driven?", Harvard Business *Review Blog.* Source: http://blogs.hbr.org/cs/2013/07/are_you_data_driven_take_a_har.html

15. Senge, P., Scharmer, C. O., Jaworski J. and Flowers, E. S., 2005, Presence, Nicholas Brearley, London, p.154.

16. Campbell, J., 1991, *Reflections on the Art of Living: A Joseph Campbell Companion,* ed., Diane K. Osbon, Harper Collins, New York, p.18.

6. ENHANCE VALUES WITH VIRTUES

I have always acted according to the principle that it is better to lose money than trust. The integrity of my promises, the belief in the value of my products and in my word of honour have always had a higher priority to me than a transitory profit.

Robert Bosch, 1921[1]

T alking about values in organisations is not unusual. Don't we all feel that despite the relevance of organisation-specific values, certain values are universal and should be part of any leadership team across cultures?

When we suggest adding virtues to values we are going 'behind' and 'beyond' the idea of values into the basic human instincts of morality that we associate with the idea of the Monk within. Virtues enhance corporate values because they tap into our common humanity with its aspiration to live a valuable, fulfilling and purposeful life. The virtues are a universal 'language' from which different descriptions of values arise. Without the virtues to guide us we are more vulnerable to integrity failures.

Virtues: the universal 'language'

In both Eastern and Western philosophy the idea of virtue has often been described as as an admirable quality that leads to a happy and flourishing life. In Buddhism, the virtues are explained as 'perfections' (pāramitā). These are described in different ways according to different Buddhist traditions but what they have in common is the belief that these are essential if we are to step out of an egocentric mentality through compassion and wisdom. In Christianity the virtues are described as 'fruits of the Spirit' such as love, joy, peace, forbearance, kindness, goodness and faithfulness. The Aristotilean and Confucian traditions refer to virtue (arête in Greek, de in Mandarin) as the mean between two extremes of behaviour: the ultimate wise balancing of one's emotions and beliefs.

The Doctrine of the Mean (中庸; zhōng yōng) is the title of one of the Four Books of Confucian philosophy and attributed to Zisi the only grandson of Confucius. This book is essentially about being aware of the need to balance one's behaviour by drawing on the virtues. The three great Confucian 'mega virtues' are ren, yi and li (but other virtues such as wisdom and trustworthiness are often included). *Ren* is the act and attitude of dealing with compassion and empathy; *yi* is the sense of justice and acting in a righteous way, and *li* covers a range of social behaviours that demonstrate respect to others and the observance of etiquettes, norms and protocols. In the Chinese classical tradition the virtues are associated with moral duty.

For the Greeks, virtue is an excellence of character or talent. Aristotle defines moral virtue as a disposition to behave well in society (even heroically) and as a mean between extremes of deficiency and excess. The principal virtues can be observed in people's behaviour and are typically the following: courage, moderation (or, self-control), justice and practical wisdom. The focus for Aristotle was not so much on duty but on living a good and flourishing life: *eudaimonia*. To flourish is to thrive in life, to experience the fulfilment of one's gifts, simple happiness, holistic wellbeing and a balanced and meaningful life.

Practising the virtues

Aristotle emphasised that the virtues are developed through practice. In other words they are cultivated by making them habits of life and putting them into action:

> For the things which we have to learn before we can do them we learn by doing: men become builders by building houses, and harpists by playing the harp. Similarly, we

become just by the practices of just actions, self-controlled by exercising self-control, and courageous by performing acts of courage.[2]

There is an implicit Suit-Monk relationship in these actions. Our inner self needs to observe and learn from the effect of our actions in the external world, from the way in which our Suit behaves and is perceived by others. Our Monk provides us with feedback intelligence about our Suit's behaviour, learns from it, and strengthens the virtues within.

The virtues are within us, not in a tangible form, perhaps, but they can be likened to small muscles that need to be exercised to grow and become useful. The virtue of justice, for example, is expressed and formed every time we respond to questions of fairness and self-interest. We see this in the very public media coverage concerning bribery and corruption, or in instances where people have taken advantage of their public position for personal gain. Public feelings can be quickly transmitted in this way, leaving governments trying to play catch-up by passing laws or taking steps to enforce laws.

In China, bribery and corruption has been a top public concern for many years and, increasingly, the Chinese government has been disciplining and prosecuting government officials who have used their position for personal gains, for their families and their friends. Pharmaceutical companies, for example, were being called to account in 2013-14 for incentivising hospital doctors to order their products.

In Europe, there has been outrage at the level of bonuses paid to bankers who are seen as putting their own self-interest before their clients and other stakeholders.

In Brazil in 2012, public appeals were being made to the courts to bring an immediate halt to the construction of the Belo Monte Dam due to widespread concerns about the impacts on affected indigenous people groups.

These are illustrations from different parts of the world that show how the innate virtues of justice and fair play are part of life. In the language of the Suited Monk, it is the virtuous sensitivity of our Monk that calls out for justice, fairplay and integrity.

Empathetic relationships

The practice of virtue takes place in our own world of relationships, not only in expressions of support for justice and self-control in the public and political domains.

In personal relationships, the classical virtues provide us with our modern word, integrity. Integrity requires us first to have a high level of self-awareness of virtues such as moderation, wisdom, justice and courage. These virtues balance (and restrain) self-interest with the interests of others. A strong concern for self-interest can become selfishness which is an egocentric orientation of the Suit in which all behaviours, decisions and activities are geared towards maximising one's pleasures and interests without respecting fairplay (justice) and responsibility towards others (moderation).

Being human, we have the capacity to be both selfish and selfless. Wise people, more often than not, manage this balance well: they are able to detach themselves and their personal interest from the good of others. In an organisational context this simply means being a good steward of resources, money, people and the environment; not exploiting one's position in the company for wrongful personal advantage.

The non-aligned Suit regards other people as means to be used to service its own needs and agenda. By contrast, a highly developed Monk has an incredible capacity for empathy with others which can result in removing self-interest from the thought process completely. The quality of empathy enables us to build constructive relationships in which we can work together for the Common Good.

Altruism describes actions that arise out of an empathy in which there is no apparent benefit flowing back to us. In fact, there are some altruistic acts that might only result in cost and pain for us. Acts of pure altruism are heralded and admired in all societies, most notably when someone sacrifices their life for others. During the horrors of war, we see stories of immense bravery and courage. The degree to which we operate altruistically is correlated with empathy, or our sense of 'connectedness' with others.

Empathy and connectedness are expressions of the universal virtue of compassion or love. Professor Daniel Batson, a social psychologist, has become well known for the empathy-altruism hypothesis, which states that 'feeling empathy for [a] person in need evokes motivation to help [that person] in which these benefits to self are not the ultimate goal of helping; they are unintended consequences.' Three of Batson's experiments were designed to test the extent to which degrees of 'empathic stress' result in altruistic behaviours. Batson and his colleagues concluded that:

1. High empathy participants will stay to help someone in distress rather than taking an easy escape from their own empathic distress.

2. High empathy participants pledged to help a victim whether or not any previous subjects in the study had pledged to help (to confirm that altruism was not a function of the desire for moral standing in a given community).

3. High empathy individuals were found to be interested in the update of a victim's circumstance whether or not there would be good news of improvement or not (to confirm that the joy a helper feels is a 'consequence, not the goal of relieving the need.')[3]

As a leader you take responsibility for making tough decisions that have to be made even though they may result in hurting others in some way. Suited Monk leaders have high empathy and can find ways of helping people to cope with the consequences of tough decisions. High empathy enables leaders to communicate effectively, honestly and with care. High empathy leaders are able to judge more accurately the response of a company's stakeholders than low empathy leaders.

Although we can think of people who seem to have a natural sense of empathy, all of us can develop this talent. It is closely connected with becoming more aware of our Monk and listening to the inner voice. Empathy develops as we practice the law of acceptance in relation to other people. We accept people for who they are. We may not naturally like a person, but we can open ourselves to them. We can open ourselves to a group of people, to a community of people and, ultimately to the whole world.

Realistically we can only cope with being empathetic to a small group of people such as family members and the circle of people with whom we work each day. As we go out to each person, accepting their unique personality and gifts, we begin to see more of the world from their perspective.

Suited Monk leaders can get alongside people and will make the effort to acknowledge the presence and contribution of different people. Managers reading this might wonder how empathising with their team members can be a realistic option when there is only time to set objectives and monitor people. Actually, practicing empathy can enable you to challenge a person in their work goals more effectively. You come at the challenges from a shared perspective, you consider the challenges they face and help them to overcome the challenges. Suited Monk leaders lead through having the right kind of conversations based on empathy.

Humility

The ability to rise above self-interest for the Common Good is another way of speaking about humility. Humility has nothing to prove: it essentially describes a person who has a true view of her/himself. A humble person can be very courageous and strong. We can immediately think of iconic world leaders who fit that description: Nelson Mandela, Mother Teresa and Muhammed Yunus. Perhaps you can think of people in your own circle who have this characteristic.

Humility means that you do not need to create a Suit to make you feel good. But neither are you shy about your achievements when asked. You don't bother about your position in the seating order around a table, or on a platform. Leading with humility means that you ensure your team benefits from the credit and rewards of success. When things don't work out, you are ready to look at your shortcomings. One of the findings made by Jim Collins in his 'Good to Great' company research into companies that outperformed the average based on stock returns was that they were led by what he termed 'Level 5 Leaders'.

According to Collins, Level 5 leaders blend extreme personal humility with intense professional will.[4]

One of the characteristics of humility is the willingness to admit mistakes and failings and not to exaggerate successes. A humble person finds joy in helping others succeed. This is a vital quality for leaders and organisations in good succession planning. Be ready to give away your work to other competent juniors. Don't cling to work for fear that you may find yourself undervalued or even redundant. A generous humble leader will not be short of new career offers.

Jochen Zeitz became well known for turning around the performance of Puma and then going on to found the Zeitz Foundation to protect vulnerable ecosystems. But despite the achievements of his Foundation, Zeitz says, 'Nobody's perfect. We make mistakes and we've got a long way to go and a lot more to do before we can start patting ourselves on the back, but it's a start.'[5] In the world of competitive business, humility is not easy to adopt when you also have the responsibility to speak proudly of your work.

The Common Good

The other virtue that fits closely with empathy and humility is the capacity to engage in projects for the Common Good. Ryuzaburo Kaku was chairman and chief executive of Canon between 1989-99. Kaku brought to

Canon the philosophy of *kyosei* which he defined as a 'spirit of cooperation' in which individuals and organizations live and work together for the Common Good. As a world business leader he was able to bring alive a spirit of practice that was rooted both in the Confucian idea of *Shuchu kiyaku* and the western idea of the Common Good.

As Kaku oversaw the global expansion of Canon he was troubled by the effects of global imbalances in trade and the inequalities of income thus created. *Kyosei* became Canon's 'most cherished principle' and was developed by Kaku as a series of stages for developing a global corporation. The first stage is simply economic survival through establishing a predictable stream of profits. For Kaku's Canon, *kyosei* meant a high quality of cooperation with employees, harmonious stakeholder relations and playing one's part in addressing global trade, income and environmental imbalances. In the visionary conclusion to his article in the Harvard Business Review of July 1997, Kaku wrote:

> *If corporations run their businesses with the sole aim of gaining more market share or earning more profits, they may well lead the world into economic, environmental and social ruin. But if they work together, in a spirit of kyosei, they can bring food to the poor, peace to war-torn areas and renewal to the natural world. It is our obligation as business leaders to join together to build a foundation for world peace and prosperity.*[6]

The same conclusions may be reached through a study of the Western conception of the Common Good but Kaku has led the way in re-conceiving the responsibility and the possibility of the multinational corporation to deliver profit and major social and developmental advances.

Almost every day we are presented with opportunities to act for a cause beyond ourselves. Often the cause in small tribal communities is to contribute to the survival and sustainability of the tribe. In developed societies, we have the chance to make a difference through giving expertise or money to a cause or helping our business to make a positive impact in the world. Being mindful and self-aware, observing and taking an interest in local and world events will allow your Monk to prompt you to contribute to the Common Good.

Companies engage in Common Good activities in different ways and for a variety of reasons. This may involve supporting a community project in a company plant, or office facility, or in actively seeking ways in which they can reduce negative environmental impacts. The increased commitment by companies to sustainability management in all aspects of trade and manufacturing is an illustration of a desire to contribute towards the Common Good – the economic benefits are not always the motivator, nor are they always apparent.

Many research studies have been conducted to explore the links that business people make between their company and serving the ideal of the Common Good. For example, Koffie Kan, a small Belgian coffee roaster, has a passion for quality coffee in which nature, product and human environment meet one another. Koffie Kan exemplifies the three characteristics of what Luk Bouckaert calls an 'inspirational entrepreneur':[7] (i) personal vocation (life calling); (ii) a passion for quality, and (iii) social commitment. These characteristics naturally flow in our life when we have found our calling and flow with it. Some of the world's largest companies today were started by such inspirational entrepreneurs.

William Lever started the company that was to become Unilever in 1885. He was motivated by the opportunity to promote hygiene through his new soap bar Iman, like Lever, wants to conduct good business for the Common Good. Unilever's Sustainable Living Plan is one example of a long term programme to preserve resources for the next generation. Polman is chair of the global taskforce for the G20 on food security and president of the Kilimanjaro Blind Trust and his reflection on these outside commitments is interesting:

> You have to get your oxygen from doing these other things, otherwise where do your ideas come from? I run marathons to raise money for this blind charity. If you don't do such things, then what's the purpose of life?[8]

This is the voice of the Monk. The Suits can take

actions when flowing from purpose. The Suit has execution capability but directed purpose comes from the Monk.

We use Koffie Kan and William Lever as examples of wise and inspirational entrepreneurs, but we could also recount the stories of many other company founders who cared for the Common Good. John Cadbury, for example, provided tea, coffee, cocoa and chocolate as an alternative to alcohol, which was believed to be one of the causes of poverty and deprivation amongst working people in the nineteenth century. Cadbury felt that he was helping to alleviate some of the misery. Following his retirement in 1861, John Cadbury devoted the rest of his life to civic and social work in Birmingham until his death in 1889. John was succeeded by his sons, Richard and George who became pioneers in industrial relations and employee welfare.

During the same period in Swizerland, Henri Nestlé, a trained pharmacist, began experimenting with various combinations of cow's milk, wheat flour and sugar in an attempt to develop an alternative source of infant nutrition for mothers who were unable to breast feed. His ultimate goal was to help combat the problem of infant mortality due to malnutrition. He launched the new product, Farine Lactée, in 1866.

A wise and inspirational entrepreneur discovers a social need and then brings business skills and innovation to meet that need. Muhammed Yunus founded the Grameen Bank in Bangladesh because he was moved by the plight of poor people who were placed in a debt bondage for their whole lives. In 1976, Yunus lent US$27 to 42 people to help them get out of overbearing debts. For Yunus, it was a moment of self realisation from which he went on to createsocial businesses which recycle profits to develop businesses for particularly marginalised social groups in South East Asia. His passion is that all companies should bring social needs and business together, summed up in the title of his book: *Creating a World Without Poverty: Social Business and the Future of Capitalism.*

The Virtue of Integrity

The Suited Monk is a harmony between a person's Suit, what they say and do, with their Monk, what they feel and value. When the Gap between Monk and Suit is closed, there is a state of integrity, meaning consistency, congruence and honesty. In contemporary English, the word integrity is often used to stand for all the best characteristics in human nature: care, compassion, honesty, respect, love, courage, justice, moderation and many more.

The single virtue that we know as justice (or *yi*, a sense of rightness in the Confucian tradition) is the sense that causes us to react to a lack of integrity. How can we work together for just and right outcomes for all if one party or more distort or hide facts that should be open for all? Most people believe in integrity as a good standard for human relationships but, in honest reflection, admit to missing the standard themselves at times due to the expediency and self-protective knee-jerk reactions from their Suit.

Congruence is the word that describes the alignment between two parties. To act with integrity, our Suit and our Monk must be in congruence: aligned and in agreement. To be precise, our Suit must line up with our true identity and character, our Monk. A non-aligned Suit can act in quick survivalist or opportunist mode without the reflective wisdom of the Monk. This incongruence is surprisingly easy to detect. Carl Rogers, a founding father of psychotherapy research, believed that all of us tend to recognise congruence and incongruence in relationships:

> *With some individuals we realize that in most areas this person not only consciously means exactly what he says, but that his deepest feelings also match what he is expressing, whether it is anger or competitiveness or affection or cooperativeness. With another individual we recognize that what he is saying is almost certainly a front, a façade. We wonder what he really feels. We wonder if he knows what he feels. We tend to be wary and cautious with such an individual.*[9]

Leading with integrity requires a genuine respect for the words we give to others, that they represent our true feelings even if in so doing we risk exposing our vulnerability, such as saying 'I don't know what we should do', or,

'I made a mistake.'

In the commercial realities of business, one's integrity is continually tested. We know of account management teams being required to sign off contracts that specify parts being manufactured in a plant in one country knowing that they will fulfil the contract with the same parts but made in another country more cheaply. It is easy to say that the customer will not notice and it will make no difference. However, in this particular case, the customer did find out and the ongoing contractual arrangements were put in jeopardy. In this case the failure to be honest at the outset resulted in a lack of trust which jeopardised future contracts between the company and the customer.

A leader's integrity may be challenged when a team's bonus relies on the reporting of certain key performance indicators. Sometimes a team can find ways of cheating the kpi's that are used to award bonuses. A failure to act consistently with one's values can quickly undermine a leader's authority and lead to distrust amongst team members. Highly efficient team operations must be matched by diligence to maintain honesty and consistency so that results achieved for the company and individuals are deserved and a trustful working environment is maintained.

At the company level integrity management needs to be integrated into the control and reporting regimes of its operations. At GE, the P&L leadership teams are responsible for embedding the essential elements of the 'integrity infrastructure' into all the business processes from small units to large divisions. Risk mitigation, audit and evaluation processes reinforce the GE philosophy of high performance with high integrity. Codes of conduct must be integrated into reporting metrics if business leaders want to effectively communicate their intent to be a company that not only talks about integrity but practices integrity in all business processes. Integrity is modelled at the top. One failing on integrity at the top is enough to signal 'flexibility' in applying integrity throughout the organisation.[10]

We need to detach our immediate sense of self-interest from a decision to 'do the right thing.' Recent experiments carried out by Shaul Shalvi and colleagues have tested people's automatic tendency to serve their self-interests, even if doing so requires acting dishonestly. They discovered that when people are given more time to think (ie not put under time pressure) they responded more honestly and refrained from lying.[11]

Our Monk wants to give voice to our virtues but our Suit often finds that voice inconvenient and will convey pressures to conform to get to quick solutions and will flag up concerns about how our stance might negatively affect personal benefits. Following the Monk's virtues, however, brings us freedom.

1. Robert Bosch, 1921, *Bosch Zünder* quoted in *Robert Bosch: His Life and Work*, Journal of Bosch History 1, Robert Bosch GmbH, Stuttgart, p.30.

2. Aristotle, 1962, *The Politics,* tr. Sinclair, T.A., Penguin Books, London, p.34

3. Batson, C. D., Batson, J.G., Slingsby, J. K., Harrell, K. L. et al, 1991, "Empathic Joy and the Empathy-Altruism Hypothesis", *Journal of Personality and Social Psychology,* 61:3, September, pp. 413-426.

4. Collins J., 2001, "Level 5 leadership: the triumph of humility and fierce resolve" *Harvard Business Review,* January (79:1) pp.67-76.

5. Zeitz, J., 2011, "A word from the founder". Zeitz Foundation website. Source: http://www.zeitzfoundation.org/index.php?page=aboutus&subpage=jochen

6. Kaku, R., 1997, "The Path of Kyosei", *Harvard Business Review,* July-August, p.66.

7. Luk Bouckaert, 2007, "Decision-making as a spiritual process", Conference speech at the Dutch Entrepreneurs Forum, 14 December.

8. Paul Polman interviewed in *Marketing,* 5 October, 2012. Source: http://www.marketingmagazine.co.uk/news/1130728/Unilevers-Paul-Polman-why-advertising-means-nothing-him-plus-vision-magic-not-metrics/

9. Rogers, C., 1961, *On Becoming a Person,* Houghton Mifflin, Boston, MA, p.342.

10. Heineman, B.W., 2008, *High Performance with High Integrity,* Harvard Business Press, Boston, MA, pp. 43-44.

11. Shalvi, S., Eldar, O. and Bereby-Meyer, Y., 2012, "Honesty Requires Time (and Lack of Justifications)", *Psychological Science,* 23:10, pp. 1264-1270.

7. TOUCH HEARTS WHEN COMMUNICATING

A leader sees greatness in other people. You can't be much of a leader if all you see is yourself.

Maya Angelou[1]

Are you sometimes frustrated that people simply do not listen and just argue their position? Have you ever felt misunderstood in a cross-cultural context or where people have different views from you and conflict arises? Have you ever tried to get your ideas across but some people are not receptive to your input or simply ignore your feedback? These are not uncommon experiences for many of us. Great leaders, however, know how to communicate effectively and touch the hearts of people.

Authentic leaders usually talk about the importance of listening to people at all levels across the company so that they can not only engage investors but also engage internal stakeholders. In fact, Chanda Kochhar, CEO of India's second-largest bank, ICICI, says that you should not just listen but absorb: 'Take in everything like a sponge, so that when you do make that final call, it's not just based on whims and fancies.'[2] To do that amongst ICICI's 60,000 employees, Ms Kochar has a formal process to reach people at each level of the organisation. Everyone has to understand your vision and the reasoning behind it and, for Ms Kochar, that means a lot of travel to regional offices and branches. She is keen to build in a discussion not only about the strategy but about how the individual can contribute.

Communicating well is a gift for some but anyone who has aligned their Suit with their Monk has a great advantage in touching hearts when communicating. When we are able to detach ourselves from our hyperactive ego, our communication will be more effective and we shall gain a better hearing.

For the Suited Monk Leader, there are four person-to-person modes of communication:

Suit-to-Suit   Suit-to-Monk

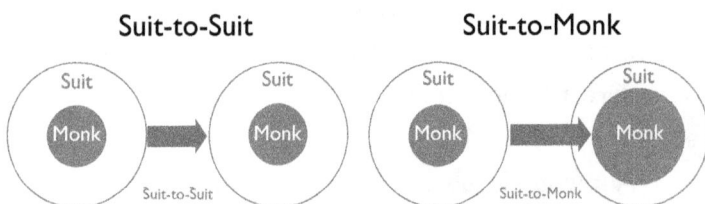

Monk-to-Suit   Monk-to-Monk

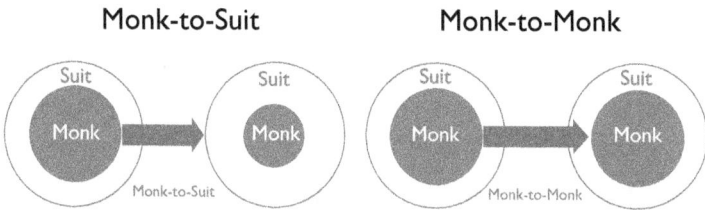

Suit-to-Suit

There are many Suit-to-Suit communication cases both positive and negative. In formal settings, where the hidden rules require a degree of role playing, using your Suit well is appropriate for positive Suit relationships. Perhaps the setting is a Black Tie Dinner where people are meeting one another either for the first time or outside their normal organisational relationships. We naturally adapt to the behavioural and conversational norms of the dinner, which may include politely listening to speeches, engaging in conversation with people we have not met before and respecting the etiquette and norms of the occasion.

In a formal professional situation you may be asked to present your business to a potential customer or client. Your Suit needs to perform well in the group so formalities are appropriate in such a process. Or it may be your first week in a new job in a new organisation where you don't know anyone and are unfamiliar with the new organisation's protocols. Your Suit is the appropriate form of engagement to help you in both introducing yourself and harmonising your behaviours. Your Suit is the form through which you adapt your conversation and behaviour for social engagement. It helps you to project your knowledge, talents and gifts into different social settings. The Suit is therefore a wonderfully flexible social identity and is helpful in the early stages of business and social relationships. Your Monk can be active as an observer of your Suit and in giving you insights in a situation.

Raf delivered a workshop on self-awareness and presentational skills for a chemical company in 2013. Part of the promotion process in this organisation involves a board presentation where the candidate puts forward ideas and concepts in a logical way. If the presentation is not successful the candidate will not be promoted. The emphasis on presenting well is high in this context so a good deal of training on presentation skills is necessary. But is that good enough to make an impressive presentation and move the audience? The answer is no. Raf recalls one of the team leaders who told one of the participants in the workshop: 'When presenting this data you can use a bit more Suit when communicating.' This was a very helpful comment; it encouraged employees to use the right amount of Suit and the right amount of Monk so that ideas are presented in a human as well as a professional way.

In Suit-to-Suit relationships your Monk should ideally be just behind your Suit so that there is no big Gap created by your Suit and your Suit can be true to yourself, avoiding the temptation to over-project yourself. Authentic leaders communicate from their Monk through their Suit.

A negative Suit-to-Suit relationship is a lose/lose relationship in which both parties are unwilling to truly understand the other's perspective and points of view. In a positive Suit-to-Suit relationship, people accept each other and are not overly attached to their own beliefs.

In negative Suit-to-Suit conversations both sender and receiver are attached to their own beliefs without being willing to listen to the other party, or open to receive input, and this results in conflict. When there is a conflict it's more difficult to operate from the Monk than the Suit. Most of the time our emotions come out and we let ego dominate our behaviour. Have you ever come across this dynamic during an argument? You realised that what you said was not correct, but you didn't want to admit it. At that moment, even though your Monk realised your position was incorrect, your ego didn't want to lose the argument. You can then give the impression of being a stubborn Suit and people may keep their distance and be less open to you.

It is precisely in this kind of context that we see the power of becoming an observer of your own behaviour. It is only when you are able to detach yourself from your emotions that space is created between your ego reaction and your true self. In that space you are able to make a different choice as you remain free from attachment to the ego, as we discussed in chapter three.

Similarly, Suit-to-Suit conflicts can occur in meetings when two Suits are not able to detach themselves from their own beliefs and thinking which then results in conflict rather than a creative openness to look for a common outcome or shared goal.

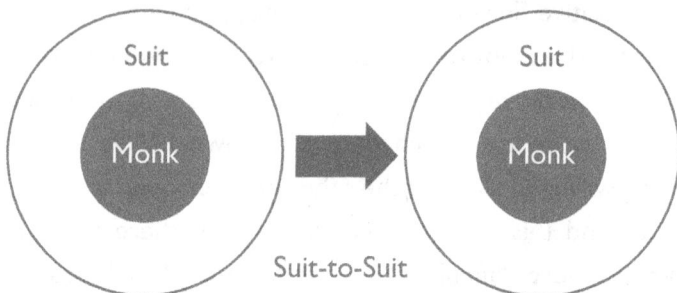

Monk-to-Suit

Monk-to-Suit communication appears when the sender is very authentic and is willing to share true emotions and feelings. In contrast the receiver is not showing authenticity. Sometimes these situations can arise unexpectedly:

- When one of your subordinates feels frustrated or unhappy because of a high workload
- When changes happen within the organisation which affect some of your team members
- When an employee didn't get a promotion or salary increase.

In these situations a person will communicate with you emotionally. Indeed, they will very likely be attached to their emotions and Suit motivators because of their frustration or unhappiness.

We recommend four strategies to help you defuse ego communication and enable the other person to calm down and communicate at a Monk-to-Suit or a Monk-to-Monk level:

1. The first key is to become aware that there is a conflict situation.

2. Be open to understanding the other person's point of view without judgment. In order to understand the other person well, you can paraphrase to make sure you have grasped what they are saying

3. Listen actively before responding; try to observe and read non-verbal cues in communication, such as body anguage and voice tonality.

4. After the other person feels that they have been understood and acknowledged, their ego doesn't feel it is being challenged. So the Monk is more likely to come out. This will help them become more receptive to new ideas.

5. Next, explore the conversation by explaining your viewpoint and ask open questions to resolve the issue. Here's an example:

> 'I can feel that you are not very satisfied with your workload. How about we talk about it so I can understand better and see if we can find a solution together.'

In this case the Suit feels acknowledged and understood and has the chance to calm down and move into a Monk-to-Monk communication mode.

In Meetings

John, a participant in one of Raf's workshops, shared that his team have a policy during meetings to help people realise when their Suit becomes too dominant and when they need to communicate more from their Monk. This team has a strong culture in general which allows them to say to someone whose Suit gets overheated, 'Hey, where is your Monk?" in a non-judgmental and humorous way. John said that suddenly people realise how they had allowed too much of their Suit in the discussion and the heat and pressure on the Suit is then lowered. This policy helps people to balance the Monk and Suit when communicating and to keep finding the best solutions in a professional and human way. A small strategy like this can make a big difference.

When things go wrong

A typical sales team discussion needs Monk-to-Monk communication to manage the Suit's defences when the team leader asks the team why sales targets have not been met. Suit defences go up and everyone applies Suit-talk to defend and explain themselves. This is the time for the leader to ask the team to use Monk-talk so the team can identify the real root causes of the missed targets rather than offer justifications about why they couldn't achieve it.

In giving negative feedback

In chapter six we discussed the importance of empathy as a virtue of the Monk. Monk-to-Monk communication means that we step into the other person's shoes with understanding which builds trust and rapport. Once the ego has calmed, then Monk-to-Monk communication is possible.

A typical example of this is in a performance feedback session in which bad news has to be delivered. The subordinate will typically raise his/her Suit to protect self-interest and defend. If the leader/feedback provider adopts a Suit-to-Suit stance, then the session will fail to achieve any performance improvement and, most likely, will further demotivate the receiver who did not feel validated, understood or fairly treated.

The person providing feedback should use their Monk to acknowledge their colleague at an emotional level aiming to build empathy. The colleague needs to feel understood in his/her own position and the feedback provider should be truthful and give constructive feedback for the recipient to improve their performance. If the feedback is based on 'political' or other hidden agenda, the feedback recipient will not activate their onk and will stay in Suit mode to respond. If, however, the initial Monk-Suit conversation can be turned into a Monk-Monk conversation, then both parties will feel good about the feedback and the feedback recipient will be motivated to improve.

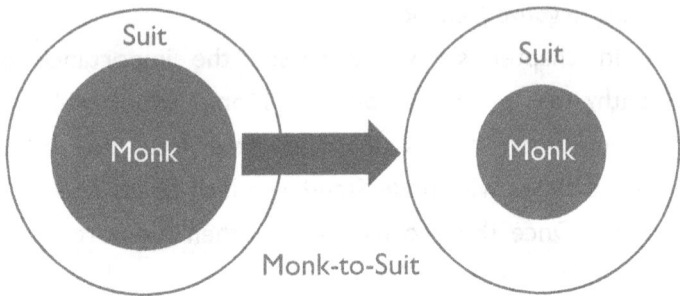

Suit-to-Monk

Leaders who adopt a Suit-to-Monk communication style can be domineering or controlling and this limits other people to release their full potential and true nature. Leaders who are attached to their own ego when communicating or giving their opinions project negative Suit behaviours towards others. Usually the Suit is brought into play out of a fear of rejection, or a fear of failure, or a fear of loss, or because the leader feels threatened. This becomes visible when leaders don't walk the talk and employees lose faith in them. Even if a leader tries to project their Monk, the followers may be unresponsive. If a leader is over attached to their own ego, they are unable to respond neutrally towards others when facing an unexpected event. As a result team motivation goes down.

The Case of Katie

One of Raf's coaching clients Katie, a team leader in Beijing, was described as having the following characteristics:

- Intelligent, fast thinking, with quick numerical analytical skills
- Sharp negotiation skills
- Aggressive, ambitious, speedy, always aiming to achieve high standards
- Proud of the characteristics which made her succeed in handling several strategic key accounts, even if it meant putting people down.

Katie was intolerant of people who thought and acted more slowly than herself. She was also intolerant of imperfect execution. Katie was also used to making decisions based on detailed data and could not tolerate uncertainty.

Katie's career goal was to be a senior sales leader of a 2,000 employee company in China. The company treasured her as a key potential talent. Since regional field sales experience of all channels is a must for being a senior sales leader, the company decided to transfer Katie from the headquarter's key account department to the largest sub-region of China as a regional sales leader. Katie knew that she was successful and had the right qualities and was one of the best performers in the region. Katie felt that she could outperform others with logic and data and she knew she was right most of the time.

The CEO of the company mentioned to Raf that he planned to launch a coaching programme as a final chance to help Katie to change. 'If she doesn't change, I am ok that she leaves the company,' he said, although he had not told that to Katie. Katie's team had a high staff turnover rate and people were demotivated. When Raf began the programme Katie mentioned to him that she felt that she was on the way to burning out.

Let's look at how a typical Gap appears for Katie

Katie

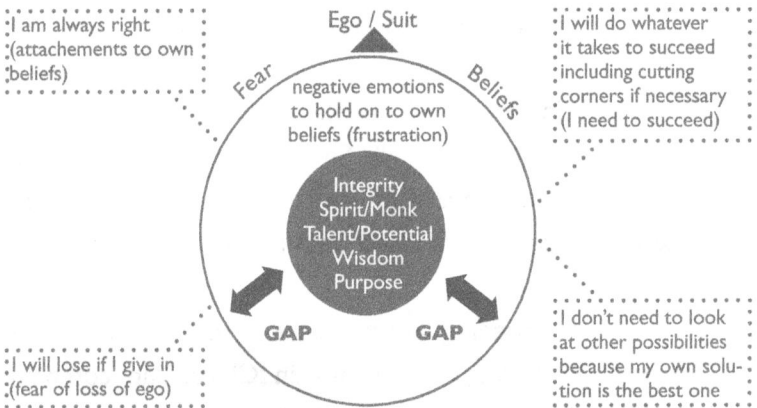

I am always right (attachements to own beliefs)

Ego / Suit

I will do whatever it takes to succeed including cutting corners if necessary (I need to succeed)

Fear

negative emotions to hold on to own beliefs (frustration)

Beliefs

Integrity
Spirit/Monk
Talent/Potential
Wisdom
Purpose

GAP   GAP

I don't need to look at other possibilities because my own solution is the best one

I will lose if I give in (fear of loss of ego)

A six-month coaching programme was introduced to help Katie go through the transition well by focusing on developing

- the ability to be more self-aware
- reduce complexity
- embrace diversity and
- build team capability instead of self-reliance

Katie was not a very open-minded person, but in the coaching session she quickly felt she was fully heard and understood (being listened to and understood transcends the ego and touches the heart).

Katie's performance at her initial three-month team integration session was amazing. She transparently shared her values, beliefs, strengths and weaknesses and even her fears (all outcomes of overcoming her own ego) and she was able to be vulnerable and look at different possibilities.

The coaching process was highly appreciated by both sides. Katie's change was witnessed by the whole company:

- She managed low performers smoothly without interfering with the team's morale
- She won her team member's admiration - many of them had doubts about her before.
- The turnover rate of her first half of 2013 was 3.8%.
- Her business result was brilliant. In the number one sales sub-region in China, her team exceeded 6% of the sales target in the 1st half of 2013. All KPIs achieved.

After these successes it was not surprising that Katie gained promotion to regional team leader.

Let's look at how Katie's Gap has changed in the way she manages herself and as a result communicates effectively with her team:

Katie

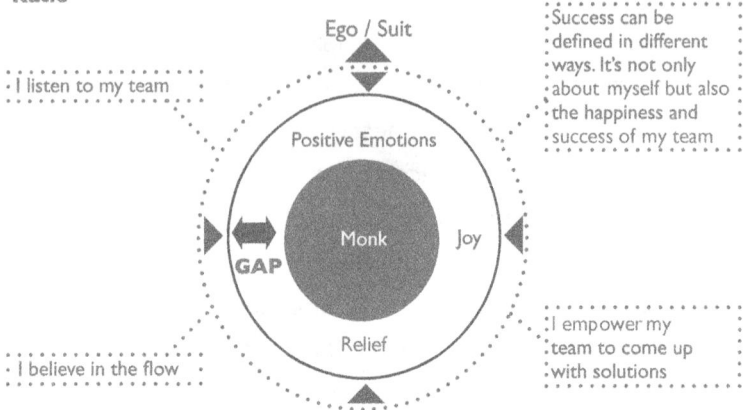

Usually when a Suit-to-Monk communication happens we first have to realise that we are attached to our Suit. This means that we are attached to our way of thinking, beliefs and our own ego. When the Suit communicates with a Monk, the Monk can actually get really hurt, because the Monk shows vulnerability and openness and the Suit projects a very direct communication style.

In order for you to have a better balance with our Suit and avoid a directive style of communication, you first need to become aware of your own Suit behaviours. If leaders are not aware of their own Suit behaviours then they usually don't have the ability to change. We don't know what we don't know. This is why in many organisations various assessments are used to help leaders realise their behavioural tendencies in different situations. Once the assessment is completed and the leader has accepted the changes that s/he needs to make then new and better behaviours can be developed. The way you project your Suit to others is in essence not who you are: it is a projection and not the real you. The good news is that your Suit can be developed; the Suit is very changeable and adaptable with the right approach by assessment, coaching and training. A well developed Suit with a good balance with the Monk will help leaders communicate more effectively and optimise their behaviours.

In a VUCA world, cross-cultural understanding is increasingly vital and we need to have the ability to learn, listen and adjust ourselves in the course of understanding and communicating effectively with one another.

The HR Vice President of a multinational organisation shared with us that most Indian leaders adopt a westernised management style by which he meant being aggressive and stealing the limelight. But he said that in Thailand business people show patience, perseverance and humility. He told Raf:

> *At one regional management meeting, an Indian manager kept talking for 40 minutes and the boss just cut him off and told him to sit down. He was very upset and came to me to complain as HR. I told him: 'You will not succeed if you stay in your 'culture box'. You do not show respect for other people and just 'preach'. You are not here to tell everyone how great you are but in the first place to listen and learn.'*

In a Chinese context feedback is not usually given directly to the Suit but given in an indirect way. In Europe negative feedback is usually addressed directly. So in different social contexts and circumstances you will have to adjust your Suit to communicate effectively.

If you want to reduce the pressure on your own Suit and enhance the Monk within when communicating with your cross-cultural team, then you can try out five practices:

1. Practice observing your Suit and become aware of your own behaviours so you can adjust your Suit behaviour when necessary.
2. Check your expectations. Make sure they are reasonable, feasible and realistic for your team.
3. Practice acceptance: different people have different views, opinions, desires and ways of doing things (culture). Respect people for their choices and ideas.
4. Pause and suspend judgement to get a deeper understanding of underlying beliefs and values.
5. Reframe your thoughts. When in conflict, look at the same situation from different angles and step into the other person's shoes.

Monk-to-Monk

Friendship gives us good examples of people

communicating Monk-to-Monk. True friends communicate without a second agenda and enjoy a higher level of trust. You can build an organisation where people communicate openly without a second agenda and build high levels of trust between colleagues and customers.

Nurturing the Monk in others is used for acknowledgement, or appreciation or a deep care for others' needs and feelings. Monk-to-Monk relationships are created by leaders who have a high level of integrity and trust and who create loyalty and engagement amongst their team. They use the Suit to get ideas across, to listen to each other's views and to look at the rational part of problem solving and data analysis. In such relationships the Gap is minimal and it promotes mutual collaboration for individuals and team.

If you look at research based on employee engagement, the highest scores when it comes to employee engagement are emotional commitment to the boss and the organisation. This emotional commitment is what we call 'nurturing the Monk within people'. Nurturing the Monk enhances emotional bonding with people, teams and the organisation. The Monk is the source of passion, engagement and motivation. A recent Gallup research survey showed that 70 per cent of employees are not engaged in their work.[3] The key element that is missing is the Monk, which is not being nurtured within people.

A leader's Suit can always get attracted by job offers from other organisations, by a better job title and more pay. But the more you nurture their Monk, the more they will be committed to you and the organisation.

There are a few prevention strategies that you can use to keep the Monk within your teams happy. Allison Rimm recommends:

> *Put in a recurring appointment — monthly or quarterly — on your calendar and ask your employees whether they are happy at work and what you can do to make them happier. Don't wait for the annual review to have this conversation.[4]*

In BASF China, one of the leaders in Guangzhou hosts a monthly gathering called 'Tea-Time' in which the team leader organises an hour and a half session to nurture the Monk within the team. Each month a new topic is chosen that is not work related. Sometimes they have a topic of family or happiness or they will talk about life's challenge. The group then has a brainstorming and discussion session on these topics to see how they can support each other. The team leader said, if one of the employees in the office is not happy and the other team members notice, they should support that person to make the person happier, or to be more understanding, or more generous, to help the person through his or her challenge or difficulty. She said that the team morale and engagement through this practice has increased significantly and there is a very high level of trust. 'Tea-Time' ignited the nurturing of their Monks and strengthened the team's relationships.

Moving forward, think about a few strategies that you can use to enhance and nurture the Monk within your people and teams to increase their happiness, engagement and motivation. A final element which enhances the Monk within people is purpose. In the next chapter we shall explore how to enhance purpose within your team and the organisation.

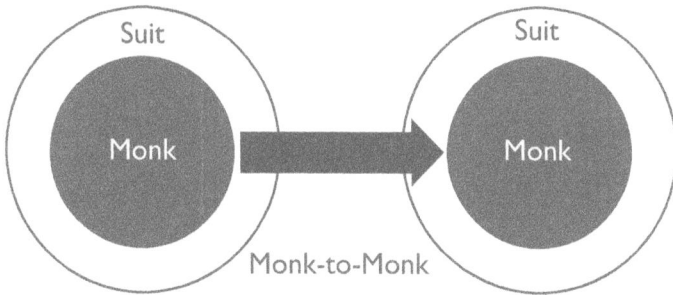

Taking some self-reflection opportunities

Reflect on a feedback session in your company and see who played Monk and Suit? What was the result?

What strategies will you apply to reduce pressure on your own Suit when communicating with others?

How can you nurture the Monk within your teams?

1. Maya Angelou interviewed by Alison Beard, *Harvard Business Review,* May 2013.

2. Clay Chandler, 2012, "Leading in the 21st century: An interview with Chanda Kochhar", McKinsey & Company Insights and Publications.

3. Source: http://www.gallup.com/strategicconsulting/163007/state-american-workplace.aspx)

4. Rimm, A., 2013, "Go Ahead: Ask Your Employees If They're Happy", *HBR Blog Network,* September 18.

8. MOTIVATE WITH PURPOSE IN LIFE AND CAREER

I know we all have our jobs, but that has to come from a deeper sense of purpose. You have to be driven by something. Leadership is not just about giving energy but it's unleashing other people's energy, which comes from buying into that sense of purpose.

But if that purpose isn't strong enough in a company, if the top doesn't walk the talk, then the rest will not last long. The key thing for CEOs is to make that a part of your operating model.

Paul Polman, CEO, Unilever[1]

Here are two questions to reflect on what motivates you in your career:

1. Do you ever feel positive energy rise up when you join a team, or are assigned a task that clearly resonates with an

idea meaningful to you, a task that will make a difference in your life or others' lives? In certain cases that may be a 'good' purpose and one in which you can make a significant positive difference.

2. Have you ever felt demotivated when routine work without meaning has not given you the platform to leverage your talents and make a difference?

From a corporate perspective, who would not like to work for a company with a clearly defined purpose to change the world? Jeff Immelt, CEO of GE, illustrates the kind of leadership that he inspires in GE:

> We have to be about big purposes... I like to remind people, if you fail here, well, what will happen? You'll leave and get a bigger job somewhere else. But if you win here, what's behind door number two? You get to be in the front seat of history, creating the future.[2]

After nearly fourteen years in the job at the time this book was published, Jeff Immelt continues to live out this vision through the innovative and world-changing work of GE.

In our experience of working with people in small and large enterprises, we have noticed that motivation shoots up when work can be aligned with a purpose that is meaningful to them and ideally links to what we referred to in chapter six as the Common Good. Most of us want to feel that we can make a positive difference to others so we find new levels of motivation when we connect with an opportunity to realise our unique purpose. Many people's primary goal for work is to make a living and support a family. The second reason is to be able to grow and learn, enhance our career and to find a sense of meaning and purpose through the work that we do. For many people, work that in itself is not motivating can become motivating through positive social relations and a strong team spirit in the workplace. Without that kind of motivation and connection to our purpose, we simply 'survive' without meaning and can become overwhelmed by the VUCA world, drifting without purpose, under-performing and giving way to a careless approach to life and work.

When we pursue purpose from our Suit

Many of us have lived without being aware of the Gap although from time to time we may have felt the reality of the Gap. We may have felt unhappy with our life and a sense that our values and talents have been underdeveloped. We may have tried different techniques to move on from a position of dissatisfaction. If you are not aware of the Gap, then self-development tends to be largely Suit-work. This means that you work on techniques, goals and exercises to boost your self-confidence, strongly projecting your Suit and, as a result, extending the Gap away from your value and purpose (your Monk).

Frank was running a successful and growing consulting firm with offices in three countries in Asia. Raf asked Frank about his ultimate purpose: 'I am going to run my business for another 10 years and then I'll be 50. Then I'll sell my business because the company will be large enough and valuable enough to sell. With the money from the sale I plan to retire and take the next step to do what I really want to do which is to find and develop renewal energy resources in Africa.'

This sounded a great idea if Frank had been already aligned with his Monk. But the reality was that Frank was not happy that he had not already realised his purpose and so was giving effort to building his Suit rather than exploring his dream. This resulted in frustration and 'unhappiness' in his workplace.

Frank's initial idea was to build a successful consulting firm but the idea did not fit with his true desire which is to develop renewable energy resources in Africa. The consulting job was a means to an end rather than a present joy or fulfilment. If the consulting firm was only a means of projecting a stronger Suit, then it is unlikely that the dream would ever be realised and this will add to Frank's 'suffering' in not realising his full potential. The question to ask is whether Frank should not directly work on his purpose and start consulting in renewable energy sources in Africa.

Have you ever worked with colleagues or bosses that 'are in the wrong place', who are not aligned with themselves? Have you ever experienced the negative impact this had on you and the organisation? Sometimes people are in jobs they don't initially like but after a few months they excel and can seem to enjoy it because they become good at it. However, it may not nurture the spirit and the dream of truly fulfilling their purpose. As a result, they may seem successful in their Suit but unhappy in their Monk. In the process the Gap increases and purpose is ignored and stress and frustration are often the result. In contrast you may have experienced work environments where people are truly happy and encouraged by a passionate boss who leads with purpose and who has aligned their Suit with their Monk. How do you feel working for such leaders?

When we pursue purpose from our Monk

Howard Schultz, the CEO of Starbucks, managed to build a dream for his company and employees. Employees do not just serve coffee, they serve an experience, the Starbucks experience. The Starbucks mission statement does not talk about their people as employees but rather partners of the organisation:

> *We're called partners, because it's not just a job, it's our passion. Together, we embrace diversity to create a place where each of us can be ourselves. We always treat each other with respect and dignity. And we hold each other to that standard.*[3]

Starbucks gives freedom and flexibility to their partners throughout their work while also bringing that freedom, flexibility and passion to the people they serve. At Starbucks, the barista takes your name and will call your name when your coffee is ready. This creates an emotional Monk connection between the barista and the customer. Not only are you externally nurtured by receiving the coffee but also your Monk through the emotional connection with the Starbucks culture and people.

When he was in his fifties, Michael Gates Gill[4] had everything he wanted: a high-paying job, a wonderful home life and good health. But then he lost it all. He was fired, his wife left him, and he was diagnosed with a slow-growing brain tumour. One day, as he sat in Starbucks, nursing a latté he could barely afford, the store manager approached him and offered him a job. The offer was made half in jest, but almost before he knew what was happening, Michael found himself in a Starbucks uniform serving coffee. Suddenly he was forced to become conscious and aware in ways he had never been before. It didn't matter that his younger co-workers lacked his level of education and work experience; he felt that they they had much to teach him about how to live life. He discovered that he derived great joy and purpose from simply serving people and brightening up their day with a cup of coffee.

All this shows how through a bigger dream and purpose, an environment is created in which employees can find their own purpose in a company that on the surface appears just to serve coffee or function as another service industry player.

Purpose driven companies outperform others

For some companies, purpose is directly derived from the impact they have on society. What is important is that this purpose is clearly defined, communicated and understood by the employees and other stakeholders of these companies. Changes, business goals and strategy need to incorporate a call for action to build this purpose.

One example of this is a medical imaging company which sells diagnostic monitors. When introducing a new product line, typically managers in the company refer to sales growth targets, bottom-line improvements but not necessarily the impact that this product would have on better diagnostics, providing higher quality healthcare to a larger number of the population - in a nutshell, saving lives. The team gets infinitely more motivated by the latter rather than focusing on the former. The reality is that usually communication to teams consists of 80 per cent rational targets and 20 per cent purpose, even though purpose is the ultimate motivator.

Raj Sisodia researched twenty eight publicly traded companies and identified eighteen companies which had outperformed the others based on characteristics such as their stated purpose, generosity of compensation, quality of customer service, investment in their communities, and impact on the environment. These were the most conscious companies — 'firms of endearment' as he terms them.[5] The eighteen publicly traded companies outperformed the S&P 500 index by a factor of 10.5 over the years 1996-2011. And why, in the end, should that be a surprise? Such companies are driven by purpose and treat their stakeholders better. As a consequence, their suppliersare happier to do business with them and employees are more engaged, productive, and likely to stay. These companies are more welcome in their communities and their customers are more satisfied and loyal.

Eccles, Ioannou, and Serafei, experts in integrated reporting at Harvard Business School, have also provided evidence that 'High Sustainability' companies significantly outperform their counterparts over the long term. They say that firms perform

> better on return on equity (ROE) and return on assets (ROA) and that this outperformance is more pronounced for firms that sell products to individuals (i.e., business to customer [B2C] companies), compete on the basis of brand and reputation, and make substantial use of natural resources.[6]

Even though your market or industry may not very obviously have a larger purpose to project, the essence of a business should be to do good as well as make profits.

Arup, the international architectural design firm with

12,000 employees worldwide in 92 countries, provides a good case study. Arup designed the Bird's Nest Olympic Stadium in Beijing, the Sydney Opera House, the Allianz Arena, the home of soccer team Bayern Munich, the Singapore Sports Hub and many more breakthrough architectural designs. Arup is an employee-owned firm and the associate said that people were proud to work for the company and they share a strong sense of ownership. As everyone is a co-owner there is less need for internal competition and politics in the organisation. There are no external shareholders who try to take the money out of the company. They invest a lot in research because 'it feels right', he said.

In 1970, Arup's founder, the engineer and philosopher Sir Ove Arup, gave a retiring speech to all employees in which he spoke about the importance of Arup's values: quality, fairness and compassion. He said: '…our lives are inextricably mixed up with those of our fellow human beings, and there can be no real happiness in isolation…'[7] Sir Ove hired people based on the right spirit and purpose. Even though profit is important for them, 'it's not our driving factor,' he said. He added, 'if you want to make money, don't become an engineer or architect, go to the stock exchange.'

When new employees join the company, they are given a copy of Sir Ove's speech. The speech has become a reference point for senior executives to stay true to the core and essence of the company. Today,

Arup's employees are engaged in humanitarian and charitable activities as a key part of their philosophy to help shape a better world.

The key insight from this story is not that the company is employee-owned but that Arup's people have a feeling of being drawn together and aligned with the values and purpose of Arup. Profit is combined with purpose.

Sharing purpose across the organisation

The good news is that companies can re-invent themselves or find purpose at their startup, provided the founders and Boards commit to reflect on what the good purpose of business means for them. Purpose, like values, should be clearly defined, communicated and understood throughout the organisation. Purpose should also be visible in organisational behaviours as much as physical infrastructure. You cannot advocate saving lives in an office space which reflects an unhealthy and unsafe environment.

Working for a company and leadership with purpose is fulfilling and can help us to self-realise. Both employees and an organisation's leadership should continually strive to embed the purpose. As leaders and their teams become more self-aware, it will become easier for them to truly identify with their purpose and also decrease tension and conflict within the organisation.

Embedding and living with purpose is a journey which may take time and reflection, involving some bumps along the way. As long as we feel the right flow we should stay on course and continue to build the dream. But if we continually experience disconnection with the purpose, or do not find the flow to self-realise in our current organisation, then we should also have the courage to admit it and consider a change of course.

Purpose is also a very powerful proposition to attract the right talents, as well as an underrated reason to align strong performing teams. Talking about purpose in the interview process will ensure that you attract talents that are aligned from the outset. It also enables the hiring manager to gain an insight into the Monk rather than the Suit of the candidate. The Suit can always be corrected and developed, but ensuring that the Monk fits your organisation's purpose is essential in securing motivation, performance and increased team spirit in the end.

On the flip side, companies usually fire people because of rational reasons: sales figures are not achieved, certain behaviours are not aligned, or perhaps certain competencies are missing. Although these may be solid reasons, they do not address the dimension of purpose and so they fail to highlight that the cause for underperformance may simply be a symptom of a lack of motivation as the employee's purpose is not aligned. By ignoring purpose, we may ultimately fire a great Monk while leaving a great Suit leader who is ultimately less aligned and frustrates her/his team leading to retention issues and higher risks for the organisation while still showing a current high performance in a rational sense.

Ultimately, if the organisation has made efforts to nurture the Monk in an employee, and has tried to motivate with purpose, and the employee remains unhappy and unable to self-realise, it may be a win-win for both to change course.

Breaking through the fears of career change

We must believe that career change is possible when we feel we're in a place where our gifts and purpose in life and work are not being realised. Sure, it's difficult. Sure, it's risky and, yes, you may lose money or status. Step one is facing these challenges with the spirit of the Monk who wants to guide you through the risks of volatility, uncertainty, complexity and ambiguity.

In chapter two we recounted the stories of Richard and Peter, both of whom were in their early 40's when they self-realised and made their 'midlife change.' They show how, with some bravery, it is possible to make a positive re-start and fight back the fears of the VUCA world. Carlo Strenger and Arie Ruttenberg explain this period of life very positively in an article they wrote in 2008 for the *Harvard Business Review* entitled 'The Existential Necessity of Midlife Change.' They say that midlife is your best chance to become the real you. Here's an extract:

Realistic programs will have to be developed to help the

growing numbers of midlife senior executives go through the long process of finding a vocation for the second half of their adult lives.

The baby boom generation is getting older, but its work is far from finished. Many people can anticipate and enjoy a second life, if not a second career. The task at hand is not as easy as the "just do it" culture of self-help promises, however. True transformation at midlife does not reside in us, waiting to emerge like the butterfly from the cocoon. Self-actualization is a work of art. It must be achieved through effort and stamina and skill. Fortunately, the life force does not just extinguish itself at age 65. Indeed, there is no period better suited to inner growth and development than midlife, when many people learn to listen to their inner selves—the necessary first step on the journey of self-realization.[9]

On the Life Journey model at the back of the book, the Suit / Ego journeys mark 'burnout' around the middle age period. Burnout, or even the stages of stress before burnout, heighten the self-awareness which leads us to listen to our inner selves – our Monk – and opens up a new stage of our 'inner journey' in which we discover more about who we are and how we want to really live our lives.

The China HR Manager for Talent Development of a multinational company shared with us one major concern she has for the company's senior leaders based on their needs assessment. She said that most of the senior leaders are very successful in their Suit, but they acknowledge that something is missing and have discussed their search for something more openly with HR professionals. Their search is the quest for meaning and purpose.

During a coaching session, Raf asked his client, the General Manager for a large American company in China, what he saw as the next step in his career. The GM's boss was leaving the company after originally joining the company with his boss. He had been working in the GM role for three years now. Should he change job because his boss was now leaving even though he loved his job? Should he wait until his new boss joined and see how s/he could help him to grow? Maybe the boss would prove difficult to work with. Should he look for a new career opportunity? But he wanted to stay in his current role for one more year because there were still opportunities for growth. At the back of his mind, the GM had a vision of becoming a business owner and told Raf that at the end of the journey of his life he would have regrets if he had never established his own business.

From time to time we all ask ourselves these questions in various ways, so what is the right thing to do? When making decisions, there are always three factors in play.

1. Challenges from your external environment. Challenges in your working environment could include: a new boss, a merger / acquisition of your company, a job relocation, a department change, new

team members, new clients and, perhaps, tension at home due to your long working hours.

2. Your internal desires, such as wanting greater freedom, more time for learning and growth, the enjoyment of working with your team, loving your job, passion for your company's product or service, or the ambition to become an entrepreneur.

3. The third element is something that most people overlook which is right timing.

Right timing is your alignment with the flow of life. The flow of life is slow, the external environment is fast. Many people get lost in business and career and lose the flow of life. There is no alignment. From the moment of conception to birth takes time. You look forward to the birth of your child but you don't know if it will be a boy or a girl, what colour hair or eyes, what kind of personality or what kind of impact s/he will have on your life. You get to know this over time; one step at a time these things are revealed. The seed is planted and everything else grows from the seed. You cannot speed up that process.

It is through 'seeds' that right timing works in harmony with you. A sudden realisation (an insight) is a seed but a realisation doesn't necessarily mean you will make a decision right away. The seed needs to grow until the time has come to change. Continuous reflection and looking at the same situation over time will gradually bring greater clarity about your seed.

In difficult times or difficult decisions your Monk will guide you. If you are not sure, exercise trust in your intuition. Many great decisions are made without thinking but when responding spontaneously to life situations.

Returning to the case of the GM, it is his self-awareness of the internal world that is critical in discerning where he is in the flow of his life. On reflection, his responses to the questions he faced were:

- I know I love my job
- Some day I would like to be an entrepreneur
- I know I want to stay in my job because there is still room for growth (he was not aware of this before the coaching so we added this to his internal desires).

When we reviewed timing in the flow of his life, two points became clear to the GM. First, he realised that he had three months until his new boss joined the company and so he would have time to see how he/she behaved, time to review his feelings about working for him/her another year. Secondly, he decided gradually to explore other opportunities, but not as a priority. He would be prepared in case things did not work out with his new boss. In this way, the GM took a pro-active approach in taking ownership of his career by planning a possible next step in advance. This career plan now becomes a seed that can grow into an opportunity. If the seed is not planted then the opportunity cannot not arise. It's only by taking action that things move and seeds grow.

We explored what may happen at the end of his career: 'If you are at the end of your career journey, is there anything that you would regret? Is there anything you need to do differently?' He concluded that he would regret not becoming an entrepreneur some day but knew that this ambition was for the future – now was not the right time. He would reflect further on the ambition in the coming year and see what would emerge, what new insight he might gain on his ambition to become an entrepreneur and consider the timing (another seed could then be planted to grow to fruition).

Peter and Richard chose to trust their Monk and the path and flow of life was revealed to them as they responded to the inner discomfort of their current situation and they were drawn by the passion and purpose of their Monks.

Taking some self-reflection questions

Do you know the purpose of your organisation today?

Do you know your own purpose in life? Ask yourself these questions:

• What motivates you at work besides external benefits?
• What would you regret at retirement age?

1. "Paul Polman talks about authenticity, transparency, a sense of purpose in business and why profit warnings don't worry him", *The Guardian*, 2 October 2013. Source:
www.theguardian.com/sustainable-business/unilver-ceo-paul-polman-purpose-profits

2. Immelt J. R. and Stewart, T. A., 2006, "Growth as a Process," *Harvard Business Review*, June.

3. Source:
www.starbucks.co.uk/about-us/company-information/mission-statement

4. Gill, M. G., 2007, *How Starbucks Saved My Life: A Son of Privilege Learns to Live Like Everyone Else*, Penguin, New York.

5. Source: http://www.firmsofendearment.com

6. Eccles, R.G., Ioannou, I. and Serafeim, G., 2013, "The Impact of Corporate Sustainability on Organizational Processes and Performance", *Harvard Business School Working Paper*, 12-035, July 29.

7. Ove Arup, 1970, *The Key Speech*, 9 July Source: rup.com/Publications/The_Key_Speech.aspx

8. Carlo Strenger and Arie Ruttenberg, 2008, "The Existential Necessity of Midlife Change", *Harvard Business Review*, February, p. 90.

9. BIG VISION - HIGH PERFORMANCE

We long for a kinder, gentler sort of capitalism — one that views us as more than mere 'consumers', one that understands the distinction between maximizing consumption and maximizing happiness, one that doesn't sacrifice the future for the present, and one that doesn't regard the earth as an inexhaustible source of natural resources.

Gary Hamel, ranked the no. 1 most influential business
thinker by the Wall Street Journal[1]

G ary Hamel's words reflect the concern and even anger felt by people East and West towards the aggressive and exploitative use of capitalism. In the second decade of the 21st century we are witnessing a significant shift in thinking and investment from a short-term, conservative risk-averse paradigm to a sustainable future which connects the business with the interests of the whole planet.

Companies like Unilever and GE have made it clear that slavery to short-sighted markets will not lead to a sustainable future for its shareholders, its stakeholders and the needs of a growing world population. Both companies have been adept at creating a new vision for their future and regularly voicing it through their CEOs. Paul Polman, Unilever's CEO since 2009, has said that 'instead of finding ways to use society and the environment to be successful, companies must contribute to society and the environment in order to sustain success.'[2] Jeff Immelt, the CEO of GE since 2001, says that 'working at GE is the art of thinking and playing big...we have to be about big purposes.'[3] A company vision is not a statement; it is the expression of a purpose and a cause in which most people in the organisation can believe. A short vision statement is only meaningful if it primarily resonates with its own people and makes sense to the many teams and departments within a company, connecting to each person's sense of purpose. It must be genuine and transparent to all stakeholders and expressed in the way a company drives its strategy and manages performance goals which connect to the idea of the Common Good, as discussed in chapter six.

When people believe in your cause and what you are trying to do for other people and society, you attract and engage the right people. But how many companies clearly state and communicate why they are in business? How many have a purpose that is 'world-involving'?

People want to be connected to a purpose; they want to be loved, nurtured, feel good, to live with purpose and to make a contribution. These desires can be found amongst employees, customers and the wider stakeholder groups touched by your company or organisation.

Big vision incorporates 'Conscious Capitalism'

John Mackey (co-founder of Whole Foods Market) and Raj Sisodia published a wonderful book in 2013 entitled *Conscious Capitalism*. They say that Conscious Capitalism is not about being virtuous or doing well by doing good according to popularised notions of 'Creating Shared Value'. Rather, they believe it is a way of thinking about business that is more conscious of its higher purpose, its impact on the world, and the relationships it has with its various constituencies and stakeholders. It reflects a deeper consciousness about why businesses exist and how they can create more value.[4]

Sadly we still hear stories every day of companies being unnecessarily small-minded. Some companies operate what we call 'Unconscious Capitalism' a kind of capitalism that builds business for personal gains rather than the Common Good. Unconscious Capitalism has no genuine empathy towards people, nor does it have a genuine commitment to preserve natural resources and social harmony

The dynamics of Unconscious Capitalism rely upon

unconscious consumerism which dictates a short-term survivalist mentality in a company's management and decision-making. This is a mindset intent on securing margin in the short-term but which is also sometimes prepared to take ethical or environmental risks or even product safety risks.

Investing in a sustainable future takes long-term vision and staying power when a Board has impatient investors and customers. This is where Unilever is an example of good practice. Their vision for the sustainable cultivation of oil palms is likely to have incurred short-term investment costs. But by 2015, Unilever's palm oil needs will be met from certified sustainable sources. In this respect Unilever has led the way in their commitment to address the ecological cost of palm oil production in Indonesia and Malaysia.

Unfortunately there are also many examples of unconscious capitalism. The need to make people redundant can be required by market changes but can be managed in a conscious way or in an unconscious way. Often it is the comparatively small behaviours of a company that belie a larger unconscious culture. Here's one example of small-minded unconscious capitalism which has embarrassed employees of Mondelez International even though the story is quite localised. UK chocolate maker, Cadbury, had a heritage of benevolence towards its workers. The company is now owned by Mondelez, one of the world's largest snack companies, with global net revenues of US$35 billion in 2012. Mondelez are obligated to put US$47 million into the Cadbury pension fund every year until 2019 to address a fund deficit. In August 2013, Mondelez announced to its 14,000 retired Cadbury workersthat they would no longer be sending annual Christmas gift boxes. The reason, they said, was due to the increasing pension costs. The estimated saving to Mondelez of stopping the Christmas pension gift boxes was US$328,000. The criticism for this action has been almost universal.

Cost-cutting is understandable in difficult economic times especially when a firm's survival is at stake. But Mondelez's survival is not at stake. Throughout the financial depressions of the twentieth century, Cadbury had managed to continue the Christmas gift box tradition. Media stories at the time of this announcement were quick to compare the cost of the gifts to the CEO's increased remuneration package that year. The sense of justice and injustice can be particularly acute in the minds of stakeholders when hearing such stories of corporate 'meanness'. The cost of the Christmas gift box for Cadbury's 14,000 retired workers was equivalent to 1.1% of the CEO's US$28.8 million remuneration in 2012. What would a wise CEO do if presented by such a situation?

Of course, this story is a far cry from more serious cases such as unsafe conditions for workers which continue in the operations of some companies and which are usually below the radar screen of publicity. Mondelez seeks to build its credibility in sustainability and good business practice through strict monitoring of its supply chains, respecting labour rights and aiming to reduce negative environmental impacts. However, management teams can lose the trust of their employees when injustice is felt if only in what might be regarded as the small issue of Christmas gift boxes for its retired workers.

When times are tough

Generally we manage organisational processes rationally, but it is our Monk that gives the organisation its spirit, mission and purpose. Hearts and minds have to work in harmony to bring both personal fulfilment and organisational success. So if you are an entrepreneur and you want to build a company or if you already have a company, think about the purpose that you serve and the value you add to society. How are you balancing purpose with profit? In difficult times it's a shared purpose and meaning that bring people together even when they have to go through the painful process of staff redundancies.

Whole Foods Market managed to maintain purpose and motivation in their workforce during a downsizing period when some layoffs had to be made. But the quality of their engagement with employees, their transparency on the company's financials and the generous severance packages and support they offered to help staff find new jobs meant that they weathered the storm with goodwill.

Trust and care are vital values for purpose to work properly. People need to know that if they share the pain of the tough times they will share the gain of the good times. Shared purpose is not a matter of getting the wording right but getting the spirit right within the culture of the organisation. This means transparency, accountability care and, in the case of Whole Food Markets – love! As John Mackey, puts it: 'Love and care are not weak virtues; they are the strongest of all human traits. Companies that operate on fear are the ones headed for extinction.'[5]

Aligning your purpose with the company's vision

Is your purpose in work and the company's vision aligned with your purpose in life? Not everyone has a clear purpose in life and in our experience many people have not identified their purpose. The search for meaning is a lifelong quest. Aligning your personal purpose with a company or organisation's purpose and vision is therefore not an easy task, but the more the two merge, the more effective you will be in your professional and personal life. Your personal purpose becomes a part of the organisation's purpose and will contribute to its vision.

Each individual in a company has a specific rational purpose and a spiritual purpose. The rational purpose of an accountant is to get the numbers right; the spiritual purpose of the person doing the work has to be discovered by the person themselves. The more the accountant's purpose is aligned with the company's purpose, the more effective both the accountant and the company will be. If they are not aligned, the more the accountant will struggle and the less the company will benefit.

We believe that finding joy in your work is possible for everyone. Ed Diener, a researcher on happiness, has found that happiness isn't highly correlated with income but it is highly correlated with social relationships and being part of a network of close connections to others. Even if the work itself is not greatly satisfying, happiness can be found in the working relationships, the shared tasks and the interactions with others with whom we work. Psychologist Amy Wrzesniewski tells the story of a hospital custodian called Luke.[6] Luke gets great satisfaction from his work, not from the cleaning and duties, but from the interactions he has with patients and their families. When Wrzesniewski interviewed college administrative assistants about their work, she found that their attitude towards work depended on how their seemingly similar work was organised and integrated into the vision of larger units of which they were a part. One of Wrzesniewski's colleagues, Barry Schwartz summarised the findings:

> If the workers had a sense of organisational purpose, and it was a purpose they could be proud to contribute to, if they had a sense of partnership, and if they had a fair degree of discretion and control, they were more likely to view what they did as a calling.[7]

If you are a team leader or a leader of an organisation, then giving people like Luke flexibility to craft their job to allow them to enjoy meaningful relationships with people can help them to find joy in their daily work. If you know why you are in business it will give meaning to your work. If you go to work only to complete the task, there is no meaning and joy.

Do you have an emotional commitment to your organisation and its products or services? If there is no purpose in the organisation then only Suit-based motivation remains to engage you in the workplace and your Monk's purpose is thwarted.

In previous chapters we have seen that everyone has a personal Gap and if the Gap is decreased we can increase the effectiveness and performance of an individual. To build a purposeful and effective organisation you need to create alignment between you and your company or organisation. This requires good communication, shared values and team commitment for long term business success.

As a leader of a team or an organisation, a vision (the dream), a mission (why your team or organisation exists), and your values (your moral character) are the heart and soul of your team or organisation. To create alignment and stability, each level of the organisation has an important function. Senior level management has the responsibility to initiate, communicate and align with team leaders on vision, mission and values, not as rational statements but as a clear reflection and agreement of a shared purpose.

Leading with Purpose and Values

Are most employees happy with your organisation? How can we achieve greater harmony in the workplace and between employees and their company? Are your people aligned around a shared purpose or why they work for your company? These are corporate Gap questions.

To close the Gap, leaders need to demonstrate a serious and authentic intent to lead a company in a way that ignites peoples' values, purpose and passion. Many people feel that they cannot lead strongly with values because they know that there are circumstances in which they will not live up to these values. Mary Gentile, the creator of the *Giving Voice to Values* educational pro-grammes, has frequently faced this question. She says that there are many times when we would like to voice and act on our values. By enabling that choice and learning to do so effectively we are likely to expand the frequency of this choice.[8] And yes, there may be times when we appear hypocritical, when our actions don't always align with words. But the common weaknesses of being human don't disappear; rather, the Monk's humble approach takes the sting out of the embarrassment of failings that the Suit feels so keenly.

Team leaders need to be able to engage their team on how individuals can best contribute to the organisation's vision. This involves one-to-one communication which gives priority to seeking to understand where the individual 'stands' in relation to the corporate purpose. Without their commitment and effort, overall performance is diluted. Keys to motivating your team are:

- Rewarding people for 'doing the right thing' in line with values, vision and purpose
- Learning to look beyond only rational outcomes to reward 'good behaviour'
- When implementing a new project, answer the 'Why?' questions. Why are you launching a new process, project or product? Share the purpose behind it – give people a reason why they should be committed and passionate about it.

These actions require some clear commitments from you, such as:

- Committing to work at ethical decisions and being open with other team members
- Being honest if bad news has to be shared
- Working alongside other team members for the bigger purpose and the organisation's vision
- Asking for help and feedback
- Withholding judgement in difficult times and taking time to search for solutions together with your team
- Closing your Gap.

When you regularly communicate purpose and values that can be accepted throughout the organisation you enhance transparency and develop cultural strength.

Developing leaders from within and recruiting good people from outside are critical tasks for the organisational leader. Aim to recruit people for their purpose, their values and integrity and not only for their skills. A skill is something you can train and develop but developing purpose and someone's values are more difficult.

In our own company, GLO, we equally assess prospective candidates on their 'Suit qualifications' and their 'Monk qualifications'. The Suit qualifications include their background, professional experience, education and language ability. The Monk assessment includes discussing the candidate's personal purpose in life, what makes them passionate about this new opportunity and what is important for them at a heart-level. We also give them a case with an integrity challenge and ask them how they would cope with it.

Closing the Corporate Gap

How can companies be authentic, believable and trustworthy? How can they make their aims for integrity actually work in practice? The corporate Suit is the identity that a company or a brand wishes to show to the world, especially the world of investors, customers and suppliers and, if possible, employees too. The written values, vision and mission are part of the corporate Suit. However, the way the values and vision are lived and acted upon by all staff and management, including the best of motives and purpose that guides them, highlights the Corporate Monk.

In earlier chapters we have seen that everyone has a personal Gap and if the Gap is decreased we can increase the effectiveness and performance of an individual. But it's not only individuals that have to work at closing the Gap. It is mutual collaboration that leads to the best outcomes in business for the individual, the team, the organisation and society. The desired outcome in building a purposeful and profitable business is to create alignment between the individual and the work team, the work team and the organisation, and the organisation and society.

The corporate Monk has a purpose. Sometimes it's clear and sometimes it's not. Purpose may emerge or be rediscovered when the corporate Suit is floundering with commercial or ethical failures – or both. The corporate Monk has values that need to be articulated by the leadership but at the same time are supported by the employees because the corporate Monk is a combination of all their values and voices.

A wise leader understands how to listen well and also how to lead in a way that motivates people with integrity and humility. As leaders deal with their own Gap closure process, so they find that a new perception emerges about what is possible with the team and the organisation. If the whole leadership team develops their Monk awareness and finds a reduction of their Gap, this will reflect in the organisation.

Building a business that creates alignment in those three areas, requires good communication, shared values and personal and team commitment for long term business success. The vision, mission and values are the heart and soul of your organisation. In order to create high organisational performance each level of the organisation has an important function in how it interacts and relates to other levels seeking alignment around a common vision.

As you communicate mission, vision and values regularly you create transparency throughout the entire organisation and create alignment from within. Alignment from within will also influence the organisational culture positively. Shared purpose will bring mutual collaboration, team effort and each individual to contribute towards a shared purpose, dream or vision. People will thrive and the company will thrive.

A big vision for 'Conscious Capitalism' at Barclays

Barclays, like many international banks, suffered huge criticism from 2008 onwards for allowing excessive egocentric actions and behaviours by some of their teams, mainly those involved in investment banking. The respectable and professional Suit of the Bank was portrayed in popular and media perception as a loutish selfish Suit, far from the professional respect that a bank requires to retain the trust of its customers and clients.

Things came to a head for Barclays when the Bank was fined US$470 million by regulators on both sides of the Atlantic for its role in rigging the interbank interest rate, Libor, between 2005 and 2009. Barclays was found to have manipulated the prices it submitted to help its own traders and rival banks' traders. In addition Barclays had to set aside U$4bn for mis-selling payment protection and make new provisions of just over US$1.3bn for mis-selling interest rate swaps to small businesses. Shareholders expressed their fury at the AGM in April 2012 and blamed the then chief executive Bob Diamond for allowing a culture of excessive speculation in the investment banking division which he headed before being appointed chief executive. In appointing Bob Diamond to chief executive in 2010, Barclays had appeared to be insensitive to the intense scrutiny of banking behaviours following the financial crisis. One British politician called him 'the great gambler' and others referred to the investment banking divisions practices as 'casino banking'. This may well have been unfair to Mr Diamond but the disgust over the payouts to bankers who had been playing for their own gain coloured the perception of those in charge. Mr Diamond had earned US$43 million in 2009.

From the Gap perspective, Barclays' attention had become focussed on making as much money as possible for traders and senior management at a level of risk that was unacceptable to shareholders and wider society.

Politicians and media voices challenged the dominance of greed in the culture of the investment banking division that ultimately allowed mis-selling and illegal manipulation of the interbank interest rate. In 2013, a further scandal was unearthed as Barclays (with other banks) was shown to have manipulated foreign currency price settings to enable clients and traders to falsely enhance returns at certain key trading points in the trading day.

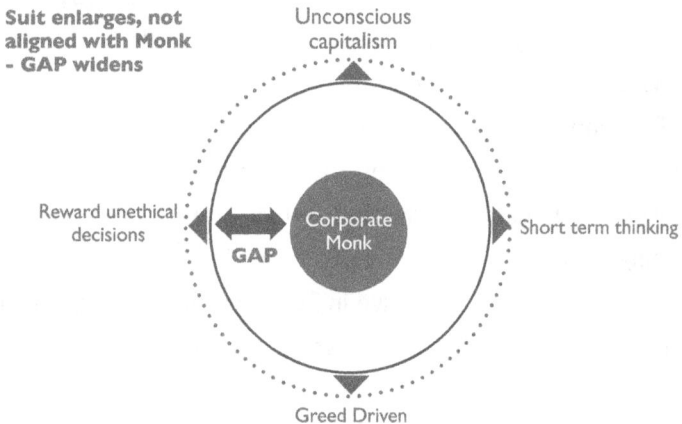

At the end of 2012, Bob Diamond and the chairman had to go. Barclays decided that Antony Jenkins, former head of Barclays' retail operations, was the man to rebuild the shattered bank where the nature of the Gap had become obvious to all. Anthony Jenkins' immediate attention was towards the neglected Barclay's Monk. He announced a set of core values to be embedded in Barclays 'at every level' and these would be included in a new performance assessment approach for senior leaders.

In a letter to Barclay's staff in January 2013, signed 'Anthony' he said that agreeing these core values was the easy part:

> The difficult challenge is to ensure we live by them. Not just most of the time, _but all of the time._ Not just for most of us, but for _everyone who works at Barclays._
>
> Over the next few weeks, we will be training over a thousand colleagues so that they are able to explain the importance of our values to every single colleague in the bank, and how they must guide us in our decisions and delivery.
>
> …We must never again be in a position of rewarding people for making the bank money in a way which is unethical or inconsistent with our values.[9]

Anthony Jenkins' intent is to close the Gap between the kind of values and purpose that most people within Barclays would like to practice but had found to be difficult in the culture that had developed in the bank, according to Mr Jenkins, over 20 years. He recognised that not everyone in Barclays would fully buy in to an approach which linked performance to the upholding of the new values: 'My message to those people is simple: Barclays is not the place for you. The rules have changed. You won't feel comfortable at Barclays and, to be frank, we won't feel comfortable with you as colleagues.' Within a few weeks of writing this, Anthony Jenkins oversaw the departures of two of the highest-paid remaining invest-ment banking heads without payoffs.

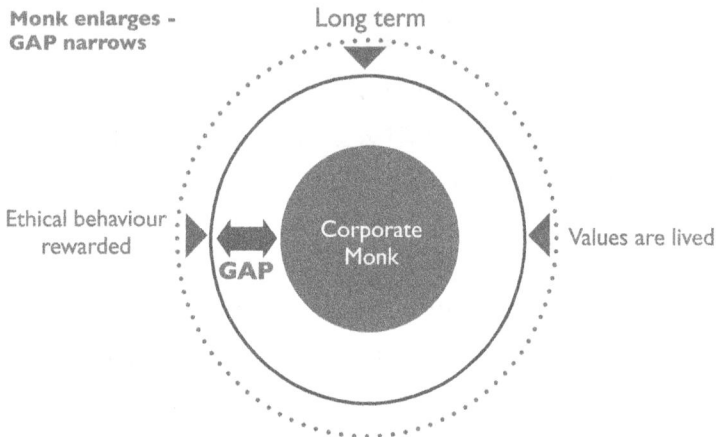

The battle to close the Gap at Barclays continues. The bank continues to deal with the fallout from the currency trading manipulation in which other banks were also involved. But the culture is changing because a leader has taken a stand on principles and values that he weights as being more important than pursuing short term at the expense of the values and reputation of Barclays. Profit-making is a good enterprise and behaving with integrity wins internal and external support. However, the payoffs for good behaviour tend to be in the long term and not in the short term. Short-term profit-making is frequently contrived at the long term opportunity cost of capital at the shareholder's expense and frequently fails to take care of the long-term consequences of tactical financial subterfuge.

Closing the Gaps in Capitalism

High profile business leaders like Dominic Barton of McKinsey and Paul Polman of Unilever are pushing for reform of capitalist markets that build short-term Suits. Withstanding budgetary expediency for longer term purpose and principles is possibly the most difficult battle for the Suited Monk CEO. S/he requires courage and risk in leading the Board to resist 'short termism'. Michael Beer and his associates at the TruePoint Center say that they have seen too many instances where the board's predominant focus on financial returns or loss of nerve in the face of predatory hedge-fund share purchases derailed the CEO's institution-building work and even resulted in the CEO being dismissed despite a strong track record of improving performance and culture transformation.[10]

Our Suits can be highly attracted by brands that make us feel good in the external world. Some companies are good at combining social purpose with their business and so try to engage their staff and customers at Suit-level and Monk-level. Ken Freeman was the former CEO of Quest Diagnostics which he took from US$350 million in market capitalisation in 1997 to US$9 billion in 2004 when he stepped down in 2004. He found ways to bring out the Monk in his company through examples and through trust-based leadership:

> *I wanted to take a company that was hostile and hierarchical, and not particularly disciplined, and create a values-oriented, honest disciplined company where the people respected each other. I had to model the behaviour at grass-roots level.*[11]

Leaders have the choice to enlarge their Monk or shrink their Monk by the behaviour they model. In turn their model can enlarge or shrink the Monk of the whole business.

Jack Ma, the founder of Alibaba, has faced a painful failure in ethical standards in his company. The scandal resulted in the dismissal of three senior executives including his friend and right-hand man, David Wei. Jack Ma gives a vivid illustration of how easy a company's Monk can shrink through failures of integrity:

> *Let's say you employ a contingent of top executives. If one day one of your best comes to you with a moral problem and you tell him he can do whatever he wants without worry, then I am sure your company will become smaller and smaller over time...It is only when everybody adheres to values, adheres to them from day one, that you will finally have a future.*[12]

Jack Ma is serious about his company getting bigger based on strengthening the internal world of its Monk.

To conclude, here are two questions for you to reflect upon.

1. Are you working for an organisation that has a vision not just limited to creating shareholder value but also making contributions to the greater good of society?

2. Would you prefer to work for a company that claims to have the best quality products bringing the highest shareholder value OR for a company that continuously innovates products to find solutions that save peoples' lives making good money in the process?

1. Hamel, G., 2012, *What Matters Now,* Jossey-Bass, San Francisco, p.31.

2. Paul Polman interviewed by *Harvard Business Review,* June 2012: "Captain Planet: An interview with Unilever CEO Paul Polman."

3. Immelt J.R. and Stewart, T.A., 2006, "Growth as a Process," *Harvard Business Review,* June.

4. Mackey, J and Sisodia, R., 2013, *Conscious Capitalism,* Harvard Business Review Press, Boston, MA, p.33.

5. *ibid,* p.225.

6. Schwartz B. and Sharpe, K., 2010, *Practical Wisdom,* Riverhead Books, New York, p.281.

7. *ibid,* p.283.

8. Gentile, M., 2010, *Giving Voice to Values,* Yale University Press, pp. 3-13.

9. Anthony Jenkins' letter to Barclays employees

10. Michael Beer, Russell Eisenstadt, Nathaniel Foote, Tobias Fredberg and Flemming Norrgreen in *Higher Ambition: How Great Leaders Create Economic and Social Value,* Harvard Business Review Press, Boston MA, 2011, p. 206.

11. Interviewed by *Strategy+Business* (Winter 2004) and quoted by Michael Beer et al op. cit.

12. Jack Ma speaking at the 2011 Annual Summit of China Green Companies reported in the China Entrepreneur Club's Green Herald, November, 2011, p. 71.

10. THE WISDOM OF A SUITED MONK

Practical wisdom is tacit knowledge acquired from experience that enables people to make prudent judgments and take actions based on the actual situation, guided by values and morals. When leaders cultivate such knowledge throughout the organisation, they will be able not only to create fresh knowledge but also to make enlightened decisions.

Ikujiro Nonaka and Hirotaka Takeuchi[1]

I n 2005, Robert E. Quinn, a professor on the cutting edge of leadership studies, organisational change and effectiveness at the University of Michigan, posed a series of practical questions that you can ask yourself about your leadership, organisation or team. The questions were designed to generate insights into the changes that we must make to become more effective leaders. The questions were:

1. 'Am I results-centred?' Have I articulated the results I want to achieve?
2. 'Am I internally directed?' Am I willing to challenge others' expectations in order to act consistently with my own values?
3. 'Am I other-focused?' Have I put my organisation's needs above my own?
4. 'Am I externally open?' Do I recognise signals suggesting the need for personal change?[2]

These are questions that Suited Monk leaders will be able to answer positively because they are self-aware, empathetic to others and able to get results without compromising on their values or purpose. These questions also bring together the Suit's need for focused management, financial performance and rational results with the inner world competencies, values and discernment of the Monk. Living out the answers to these Monk-directed questions requires an alignment between your Monk and your Suit. In this chapter, we explore the wonderful faculty of wisdom which we can enjoy when our Monk is aligned to our Suit.

The Wisdom Project

During 2010-2012, Mike led the Wisdom Project at

the China Europe International Business School (CEIBS) to research the way wisdom was understood in the practice of managerial decision-making. Decision-making in the complexity of business life can never be a perfect art. But when managers are able to transcend their own self-interest for the sake of their responsibility to their organisation and its stakeholders, aspiring to do the right thing, then they are admired for their character and not just their performance.

In the VUCA world, business decision-making is complex, especially when plans don't work out and alternative plans have to be put into place at speed. Statistical techniques are prone to estimation errors and data points may be incomplete, or even non-existent, despite the ever-increasing reliance on 'Big Data'. Investment decision-making is also complex. Analytical modelling used to assess the risk of losses in a portfolio is less secure than once believed. In the midst of the VUCA world, managers need wisdom to respond to complexity and uncertainty with consideration for the human factors within and beyond the organisation. This is what it means to exercise wisdom in leadership. But what, then, does wisdom really mean?

Wisdom psychologists, Baltes and Staudinger, say wisdom is 'expert knowledge in the pragmatics of life' and we could point to a range of research studies in experimental psychology to support their definition.[3] They further show that wise people can transcend egocentric behaviours to promote the Common Good.

Baltes and Staudinger have shown that wisdom is linked to insight and virtue and also to personality characteristics such as maturity, absence of emotional liability, open-mindedness, even-temperedness, and sociability.[4] Other psychologists have shown that wise people deal effectively with uncertainty and ambiguity and are more emotionally stable than the average person.[5]

Wisdom is both a human faculty and a practice that has, over the centuries, been explained in psychological, philosophical and spiritual terms. Health psychologist, Professor Carolyn Aldwin, has summarised wisdom as a practice

> that reflects the developmental process by which individuals increase in self-knowledge, self-integration, nonattachment, self-transcendence, and compassion, as well as a deeper understanding of life. This practice involves better self-regulation and ethical choices, resulting in greater good for oneself and others.[6]

The questions which we used for the Wisdom Project focused on managerial decision-making and the application of wisdom in business. The Wisdom Project research involved consultations with 184 senior executives, 96 based in China and 88 from twenty two other countries. Most of the respondents worked in commercial organisations at the most senior levels. Management has often been regarded as a fact-based scientific undertaking, and managerial decision-making requires knowledge and a rational approach, so respondents were asked if they could describe how, in their experience, wisdom might add something more to the decision-making process. The executives' responses generated 18,000 wise words which were analysed and mapped.

When the most commonly-used phrases and ideas were grouped together, it became clear that the complexity of wisdom could be visualised as a three-dimensional prism with three clusters of human capacities: Rational Capability, Intuitive Insight and Humane Character. A number of psychologists have identified closely related traits of wisdom, namely emotional and behavioural regulation and the ability to deal effectively with ambiguity and uncertainty. We have called these elements 'Emotional Stability', which we view as a psychological foundation for the clusters of wisdom illustrated by the Wisdom Prism. At the heart of all these dimensions is the capacity for self-awareness which is the work of our Monk.

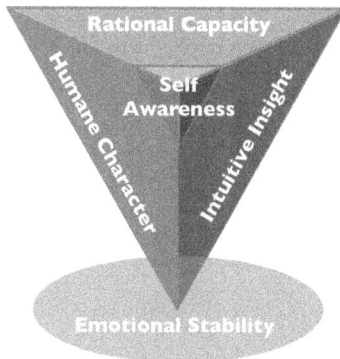

Rational Capability

Wise managers are competent in reading and analysing data objectively and rationally to inform quality decision-making. Executives in the Wisdom Project survey spoke about how wisdom helps them with the rational processes involved in making quality decisions. For example, the GM of a Portuguese bathroom company told us:

> *Based on knowledge/ration and intuition/emotion, wisdom is the general understanding of the complexity of circumstances beyond pure rational thinking and the use of experience/lessons learned in an intelligent way in any future circumstances.*

Wise people use their rational capability well. This means that they use statistical algorithms, formulas or verified modelling to process information free from biases to reach decision-making. Daniel Kahneman, the Nobel prize-winning psychologist, warns that 'humans are incorrigibly inconsistent in making summary judgments of complex information.'[7] Leaders are required to develop rigorous practices which spot facts and details; being aware of our rational capability and using it correctly is the mark of wisdom.

The Wisdom Project revealed that executive leaders understand wise decision-making to be a blend of logical fact-based thinking, intuitive insight and a heightened moral awareness creating character marked by integrity. The COO of a branding agency described the ingredients of wisdom as: 'experience, knowledge, maturity and multiple forms of intelligence: intuition, spirit, heart, reason.'

Intuitive Insight

In chapter four we described intuitive insight as a 'sight from within' and we gave examples of entrepreneurs and business people who can see or sense ahead both opportunities and risks that are not observable through the normal working with data analytics. Our Monk is the source of intuitive insight or what some call 'gut instinct'. The nature and validity of intuition has been long debated. Daniel Kahneman argues that valid intuition can only be related to expertise and skill and an environment that is sufficiently regular to be predictable.

Whatever the cause or explanation for what we call intuition, we recognise the concepts of 'insight' and 'instinct'. From the responses given by the executives who took part in the Wisdom Project survey, descriptions of intuition, gut instinct and insight were widespread. In the mapping process we found that data, facts, information, rationality and business were one cluster of words associated with managerial decision-making but this was balanced by words associated with intuitive insight. The importance of balance between these two fields of wisdom was made explicit in the comments made by two Chinese executives who said that information, data and a rational approach are 'useless' and 'insufficient'.

What emerged in the survey data was the power of intuition as a hallmark of wisdom. Here are the thoughts of two more survey respondents:

> *Wisdom is close to intuition. Insight into what might happen in the future. It combines intuition with logic and applied common sense.*
>
> VP of a Biofuels company

> *In my view, wisdom, much like intuition or 'gut feeling', [is] being able to consciously or unconsciously apply rules, priorities, principles, experiences and other relevant knowledge, presenting them in a fashion that provides focus and insight to the present decision to be made. In my view, intuition, gut feel and wisdom is, in many cases, the unconscious application of patterns that we connect to the present matter at hand.*
>
> Global Head of Information Services and Compliance Company

Intuitive instincts require checking wherever possible – primarily with known data points and knowledge using one's rational capability. Being aware of the limits of one's prejudices, biases and expertise is also part of the rational balance to intuitive judgements. But in the twenty-first century there has been a greater willingness to recognise that intuition and the sense of self is not fully explained by cerebral reason or scientific knowledge alone. Science can only measure behaviours not what people refer to as 'gut instinct'. According to Aristotle, wisdom requires intuition and scientific knowledge.

Making wise decisions requires a good reading of your environment and a quality assessment of the opportunities that you see – and patience. Intuition, trusting the flow of life and using your rational capability, is a key to making wise decisions.

Humane Character

Character is the inner world and nature of our Monk – the kind of people we are and the values and purpose we live by. Being humane means living with the tension of following our own self-interest whilst considering others and living for the Common Good. As Meeks and Jeste have pointed out in their study on the neurobiology of wisdom:

One of the most consistent subcomponents of wisdom, from both ancient and modern literature, is the promotion of common good and rising above self-interests, ie, exhibiting prosocial attitudes and behaviors, such as empathy, social cooperation, and altruism.[8]

213

Shaul Shalvi and his colleagues have gathered research findings that suggest that people's automatic tendency is to serve their self-interest, a tendency people can only overcome when they are able to exert self control.[9] In our terminology, the nature of the Suit will instinctively seek self-interest first. But pausing to listen to the Monk within enables us to balance a decision with self-control.

Being humane describes all the best characteristics of human nature: care, compassion, respect, integrity, love, courage, justice and moderation. In short: goodness. The classical economist, Adam Smith, called it 'fellow-feeling'[10] which combines the ideals of empathy and the Common Good. Wisdom psychologists call it 'self transcendence' and foundational to all measures of wisdom. Robert Sternberg says that

> Wisdom is involved when practical intelligence is applied to maximizing not just one's own or someone else's self-interest, but rather a balance of various self-interests (intrapersonal) with the interests of others (interpersonal) and of other aspects of the context in which one lives (extrapersonal), such as one's city or country or environment or even God.[11]

This ability to manage these interests is the key to answering Quinn's leadership question positively, 'Am I other-focused?' Again we return to a theme in the story of the Suited Monk: when our Monk is truly aligned with our

Suit, then our perception of self-interest changes because it is no longer driven by egoic drives but rather views the external world from the perspective of fellow-feeling.

This fellow-feeling impulse was well-expressed by a Russian General Manager in the Wisdom Project survey who commented that 'a wise person is a kind one, not a saint but ethical, with high morals, his personal values are human oriented, more listening than speaking.' The Wisdom Project identified a particularly strong emphasis on the wise leader's capacity to overcome personal self-interest and pride with humility as a wise virtue frequently mentioned by the respondents.

Humane character is actually a process rather than a state. We follow the lead of our Monk in becoming who we truly should be and the sense of fellow feeling is really another way of describing the path of 'flourishment'[12] in which we more consistently and unconsciously practice the virtues of humanity that we discussed in the previous chapter.

Emotional Stability

When it comes to making decisions under pressure, people look for leaders to hold their nerve and to remain calm and controlled even when people around them are succumbing to emotional outbursts of different kinds. Emotional stability is both born and made. Some people are, by nature, more emotionally volatile than others; each person's mix of neurotransmitters is unique. For some of us, maintaining 'impulse control' is more difficult than for others. But as we work on the disciplines for closing the Gap that we outlined in chapter three, so emotional stability grows.

Emotional stability is the result of truly accepting the circumstance in which we find ourselves. Some people are admired for keeping their steely nerve in crisis situations; they are able to exert emotional regulation for the task. Wise decision-making depends on detaching one's personal emotions and impulses when emotions around are running high. From her psychological research studies, Monika Ardelt says that this means an 'absence of indifferent or negative emotions toward others, and remaining positive in the face of adversity' and that wisdom 'includes awareness of life's inherent uncertainty yet the ability to make decisions in spite of this.'[13] The most readily expressed negative emotions are fear and anger. We are not advocating a suppression of anger and fear, but rather the developmental process towards a position in life where anger or fear cease to exist. Even if that state is not possible all of the time, we believe that it is possible for us to live in a peaceful and emotionally stable state for most of the time.

We need to return to the Gap model to understand how we can deal with the causes that underlie emotional instability. The greater the Gap between our Monk and our Suit, the greater is the potential for emotional instability.

Fear arises when our Suit demands certainty and pushes to gain certainty either at the expense of others or at the expense of one's personal peace, or at the expense of both self and others.

The Law of Rejection that we outlined in chapter two is a cause of emotional instability. When we reject a situation that is facing us, such as the possibility of losing our job, or not finding one, the uncertainty leads to an internal struggle. We may react to the situation and then become fearful of what might happen to us: of losing face, of losing status, of losing friends or loved ones. These fears arise from the mind and, sadly, by giving room to such fears we are less able to live positively and the fears can then dominate our thought processes. The Law of Acceptance tells us to 'step beyond' the immediate situation, as though we could look down on it from above, to view ourselves and our reactions from a different perspective – from the Monk's perspective. This is an especially difficult act for those who have a more 'driven' temperament. We feel we have to keep pressing on to find the way and that standing still is an inadequate, or an impossible, response.

The natural state of the Monk is true happiness. The impulse of our minds is to continually search for security in the external world: finance, a useful network and a range of material and lifestyle comforts that are seen to be appropriate to our needs and interests. Take money as an example. One of the most basic survival instincts we have is to have enough money to meet our needs. What if your source of income is coming to an end, as a result of the end of an employment contract, for example? This could be a very valid reason for you to lose emotional stability. Naturally you will feel anxious and possibly fearful about what the future may hold for you and your family without any income. If you have been largely living on 'Suit energy', then you will be frantically trying anything you can to get work – ideally well-paid work. Your Suit's desperation for external security will drive you to get immediate resolution to the angst created by lack of finance. Sometimes frenetic activity brings results, but sometimes the short-term gains for peace of mind are at the expense of longer term life fulfilment.

There are no rules, but as we get to know our own Monk better, we can give greater trust to the instincts from our internal world. Whereas the Suit will give reasons to pursue a range of actions to find a way through to getting another job, the Monk may have a different sense of the best course to follow your life purpose. Almost always, following the Monk's 'voice' involves risk from the perspective of our Suit. The Monk may also give you reflections and options that do not match the demands of your Suit, such as the joy of living without the usual 'baggage'. So the Monk inside you may say, 'rent or sell your home, sell your car, become a student again, maybe move to a completely new and lower cost location.' When your Suit aligns to the voice of the Monk you can really feel energised by the power of that alignment and less anxious and fearful.

If you give time and space to listen to your Monk, you will find that ideas will come into your mind that you had not thought of before, or that build on some ideas that you have had in the past but did not develop. We have both found ideas for developing our career journeys which came through what seem to be unprompted ideas. We mentioned Mike's 'call' to Shanghai in October 2008, the same year that Raf felt the impression that he should move to Shanghai, following Raf's expat job being terminated in South China just before the financial crisis. Raf's intuition guided him to go to Shanghai in October 2008. This was a completely unexpected move but resulted in a strong friendship and business relationship.

Of course the ideas that come into our minds need to be tested and held for a little time to check how strong the feeling is and also to explore the practicalities involved in following through on the idea. This was the case for Henry in Lagos (chapter four) who flipped the coin in June 2013 but then spent many months weighing up the implications before launching his new career in April 2014.

The Suited Monk Way to Wisdom

In the Wisdom Project survey we asked executives: 'How does one acquire wisdom?' Most referred to learning, practice, experience, learning from mistakes, insights, listening and observing. A number of executives in the survey spoke about the reflective process in acquiring wisdom:

- An Austrian GM mentioned experience but also what he called 'the faster track - listen to your inner self'
- A UK Change Manager said that it was 'through listening, watching and observation,' but also, 'through acknowledging one's instinct and asking internally for direction'
- A Chinese Communications Director said: 'Follow your heart'

These three responses are examples of people who when asked about acquiring wisdom referred to their internal world. There is a listening from within but there is also a reflection process for 'insights' and a time to learn by really listening to others and observing. As we interact with the external world, our Monk observes, absorbs and learns. Our Suit gains experience and confidence from making mistakes as well as successes. In harmony Suited Monks can grow in practical wisdom and blend the discipline of practice - both of skills and the character virtues.

It is easy to forget the childhood leaps of learning in which we had to trust our bodies to ultimately line up with what our instincts led us to do:

To crawl
To stand without being aided
To take our very first step
To balance on a bike for the first time
To catch a ball for the first time

In each of these basic childhood experiences, we had to trust our instincts, senses, vision and balance. There were no formulas to learn. Rather the activity flowed from instincts that we trusted despite falling over or missing the ball many times. We kept going until we walked, talked, cycled and maybe swam too. In childhood, we were therefore more naturally Monks than Suits. We trusted our instincts. The Suited Monk way to purposeful living and leading is to keep developing trust in our instincts, our perceptions, our feelings and to appropriately use our minds and rational processes to respond to the external world via the Suits that we wear. In the words of psychiatrist, Carl Rogers:

> *Time and again in my clients, I have seen simple people become significant and creative in their own spheres, as they have developed more trust of the processes going on within themselves, and have dared to feel their own feelings, live by values which they discover within, and express themselves in their own unique ways.*[14]

Wise leaders are self-aware: aware of their prejudices, their social conditioning and thus able to moderate the tendency to be over-optimistic with their intuitive instincts. But they have also learned to value intuition, having learned to use it well in combination with their rational capability and experience. We grow in wisdom as the Gap between Suit and Monk closes. We live in acceptance of who we really are. We are not easily rattled by the foibles and failings of ourselves and others. We connect better to others because our Monk shines through our Suit rather than being buried and undeveloped within. The quality of our decision-making improves in teams because we develop a capacity to detach ourselves from the emotions and the politics of decision-making to judge for the Common Good and to restrain our self-interest.

Leading Wisely as a Suited Monk

There are many models of leadership with a distinguished track record of helping leaders to develop. The Servant Leadership model first developed by Robert Greenleaf has accompanied shifts in Western leadership models away from 'command and control' towards sharing power and considering the needs of others first to build a high performing organisation.

Transformational leadership models have been widely embraced by organisations and management development programmes. Transformational leaders are characterised by high levels of inspiration, integrity, selflessness, knowledge and talent, and proaction (M. DeVivo, 2012[15]). Transformational leaders foster empowerment and self-determination, which generate high levels of commitment (Avolio et al., 2004[16]). Authentic leadership emphasises the importance of values and empathy. In the words of Harvey, Martinko and Gardner, authentic leaders 'possess self-awareness of, and act in accordance with, their values, thoughts, emotions, and beliefs.'[17]

The wisdom of Suited Monk Leaders brings a fresh perspective to these leadership models in ten ways. Suited Monk Leaders:

1. Make decisions by establishing facts and using logical processes combined with intuitive insights
2. Develop imagination and foresight, with the actions of humane character
3. Encourage intuitive thinking, imagination, creativity and innovation
4. Encourage their teams to self-realise and to find true happiness in career and life
5. Practice Monk-to-Monk communication which touches hearts, focusing the message on what motivates the respondent
6. Pursue a vision of the Common Good to do good for society at large as well as for their organisation
7. Work with others in humility and integrity
8. Lead with emotional stability

9. Work with the energy of flow to navigate their way through the VUCA world, and,

10. Achieve high-performance with teams aligned around a shared purpose and vision.

1. Nonaka I. and Takeuchi, H., 2011, "The Wise Leader", *Harvard Business Review*, May, p. 60.

2. Quinn, R. E., 2005, "Moments of Greatness: Entering the Fundamental State of Leadership", *Harvard Business Review, August*, pp 75-83.

3. Ethan Kross and Igor Grossmann, for example, list eight studies that describe the forms of pragmatic reasoning and behaviour that help people to navigate life's challenges and is characterised by the capacity to transcend egocentric viewpoints with a prosocial orientation that promotes the 'common good.' (Kross E. and Grossmann, I., 2012, "Boosting Wisdom: Distance From the Self Enhances Wise Reasoning, Attitudes, and Behavior", *Journal of Experimental Psychology*, Vol. 141, No. 1, p.43).

4. Staudinger, U. M., Lopez D. F., and Baltes, P. B., 1997, "The Psychometric Location of Wisdom-Related Performance: Intelligence, Personality, and more?", *Personality Social Psychology Bulletin*, 23, p.1201.

5. Meeks and Jeste have provided an overview based on their interpretation of the literature on wisdom categorised under six headings: (1) Prosocial attitudes and behaviours; (2) Social decision making/pragmatic knowledge of life; (3) Emotional homeostasis; (4) Reflection/self-understanding; (5) Value relativism/tolerance, and, (6) Acknowledgment of and dealing effectively with uncertainty and ambiguity. Meeks T.W. and Jeste D.V., 2009, "Neurobiology of Wisdom: A Literature Overview", *Archives of General Psychiatry*, 66:4, p. 356.

6. Aldwin, C. M., 2009, "Gender and wisdom: A brief overview", *Research in Human Development*, 6, p.3.

7. Kahneman, D., 2011, *Thinking, Fast and Slow*, Penguin Books, London, p.224.

8. Meeks T.W. and Jeste D. V., 2009, "Neurobiology of Wisdom: A Literature Overview", *Archives of General Psychiatry*, 66:4, p. 357.

9. For the full research citations used to support the use of self-control over self-interest, see Shalvi, S., Eldar, O. and Bereby-Meyer, Y., 2013, "Honesty requires

time (and lack of justifications)", *Psychological Science,* 23:10, pp. 1264-1270.

10. Adam Smith explains fellow-feeling in his *The Theory of Moral Sentiments* (1759/2009, Penguin Books, London, p.15): 'Whatever is the passion which arises from any object in the person principally concerned, an analogous emotion springs up, at the thought of the situation, in the breast of every attentive spectator.'

11. Sternberg, R. J., 1998, "A Balance Theory of Wisdom", *Review of General Psychology,* 2(4), p.354.

12. In "*Homo Spiritualis* in Business", Mike uses, 'flourishment' 'to capture a group of inter-related notions which include: an optimistic spirit of growth; fulfilment of one's gifts; simple happiness; wholistic wellbeing and a balanced and meaningful life. ... In short, to flourish is to thrive in life and can include both economic and spiritual prosperity. Flourishment can flow within the individual and in global business through living out the virtues, having a sense of ultimate purpose and a commitment to quality.' (In Bouckaert, L. and Zsolnai, L., eds., 2007, *Spirituality as a Public Good,* Garant, Antwerp, pp. 35-52).

13. Ardelt M., 2004, "Wisdom as expert knowledge system: a critical review of a contemporary operationalization of an ancient concept", *Human Development,* 47(5), pp. 257- 285.

14. Carl R. Rogers, 1961, *On Becoming a Person,* Houghton Mifflin, Boston, MA, p.175.

15. DeVivo, M., 2012, "Transformational Leadership, Responsible Tourism, and Sustainable Development" in a paper presented to *Africa Leads: 2nd International Conference on Responsible Leadership,* University of Stellenbosch Business School, 19-21 November, 2012.

16. Avolio, Bruce J., et al., 2004, "Transformational leadership and organizational commitment: Mediating role of psychological empowerment and moderating role of structural distance", *Journal of Organizational Behavior* 25.8, pp. 951-968.

17. Harvey, Paul, Mark J. Martinko, and William L. Gardner, 2006, "Promoting authentic behavior in organizations: An attributional perspective", *Journal of Leadership & Organizational Studies* 12.3, pp.1-11.

EPILOGUE

The mind of a leader must be free - a mind that can dream and imagine. All new things were born in dreams. A leader must have the courage to be a nonconformist, just like a scientist. He must dream even if he dreams alone or if people laugh at him. He must not let his heart falter.

Shimon Peres[1]

These inspiring words by Shimon Peres, the former President of Israel, touch the essence of our account of Suited Monk Leadership. The words represent the call of the Monk which is the freedom to encourage the formation of dreams and to follow them; to respond to the fears of the Suit when contemplating the risks of following with courage and integrity; and to overcome the pressure to conform whilst at the same time offering diligent service to those we lead and those we serve. In short, they highlight the call to see our Suit empowered, guided and inspired by the passion and dreams of our Monk.

In a volatile, uncertain, complex and ambiguous world, nothing external is certain. But we can enjoy stability within by the way we navigate ourselves through the VUCA world to live a good life in which our dreams are allowed to flow so that our talents and gifts are aligned through the great projects that will come to us on our life journey.

By being true to yourself - through closing the Gap between your Suit and your Monk - we believe that you can become a more authentic leader. People will find inspiration in your spirit and dreams; they will be encouraged to discover their own dreams and purpose and they will follow your lead with a sense of vision and direction. As you align your Suit with your Monk, you will give hope, courage and a vision for the good of society through work – whatever shape that work might take.

Every leader can make a difference. Organisations consist of individuals that together make a difference. Societies consist of organisations and communities that make a difference. Social media can now assist in highlighting the good and exposing the bad faster than ever before. Leaders can no longer hide behind the established culture of an organisation; our virtually networked world exposes behaviours of individual leaders and not just organisations. Organisational culture needs to be sustained every day in all the actions and communications of its leadership team. The Suited Monk Leader is well-equipped to meet these challenges, to rise above petty self-posturing and a fearful concern for self interest. The Suited Monk Leader is a leader of poise and gravitas as well as a humble leader.

The VUCA world needs wise leaders who not only rely on 'fact-based thinking' but also on their own self awareness, intuitive thinking and ethical behaviour. They understand their strengths and weaknesses, their moods and temperament, and manage themselves from the peace of their Monk.

The way of the Suited Monk is healthy, keeping us free from the physiological and psychological damage of acute stress and burnout. The shift in the business climate to much greater awareness of the need for integrity and ethics is a call to the Monks in us to grow - a call to close the Gap between over-extended egos and authentic living and leading.

We have suggested a way in which you can live and make decisions from your Monk. We believe that you will see the benefits in your personal wellbeing and in the relationships with your family and friends. You will gradually move towards the work that you were born to do and your work performance will improve. As you take your time to move peacefully through the journey of your career, rather than treating it as a race, you will enjoy the journey much more. It will become a joy to work without the pressure to keep succeeding quickly.

We are aware that our contribution to the vast knowledge and practice of leadership is extremely modest. We are also aware that by writing about the Flow and the virtues of the Monk we are touching on spiritual themes which lie undeveloped by us. Whatever our individual life purpose may be, we cannot help but believe that there is a larger purpose for all of us along life's journey. Professor Stanley Hauerwas, in his Gifford Lectures in 2001, spoke about working 'with the grain of the universe'. That is a simple and yet mysterious idea. We find our interconnectedness as human beings within a greater connectedness. There are profound truths to do with purpose and identity in the idea of our lives working with 'the grain of the universe.'

Our hope in writing this book is that we have been able to connect with and touch your Monk and your Suit so that you will be even better equipped to make the best decisions, to lead well and to enjoy your life journey.

We wish you joy amongst all the challenges of living your life to its full purpose.

1. Shimon Peres, President of Israel, in an interview with Rik Kirkland for McKinsey Insights and Publications, September, 2012. Source: http://www.mckinsey.com/insights/leading_in_the_21st_century/an_interview_with_shimon_peres

THE AUTHORS

Raf Adams

Raf is a speaker and executive coach focusing on self-mastery and authenticity in corporate and personal life. Since 2009, Raf has led Suited Monk Leadership workshops including executive coaching for international companies such as BASF, BP, Philips, Bayer and Mead Johnson. Raf is the author of *The Suited Monk: Finding Your Life's Purpose And True Happiness* and is Chief Wisdom Officer at GLO - Good Leaders Online.

Dr Mike J. Thompson

Mike has served alongside entrepreneurs throughout his career. His business academic career has focused on responsible leadership and corporate governance, most recently as a faculty professor with the China Europe International Business School (CEIBS). Mike serves on the boards of GLO - Good Leaders Online, GoodBrand, the sustainable enterprise consultancy and Impact Hub Kings Cross, London. Mike's most recent book is: *Wise Management in Organisational Complexity* (edited with David Bevan).

THE LIFE JOURNEY MODEL ®

From the book "The Suited Monk: Finding Your Life's Purpose And True Happiness" available at www.amazon.com

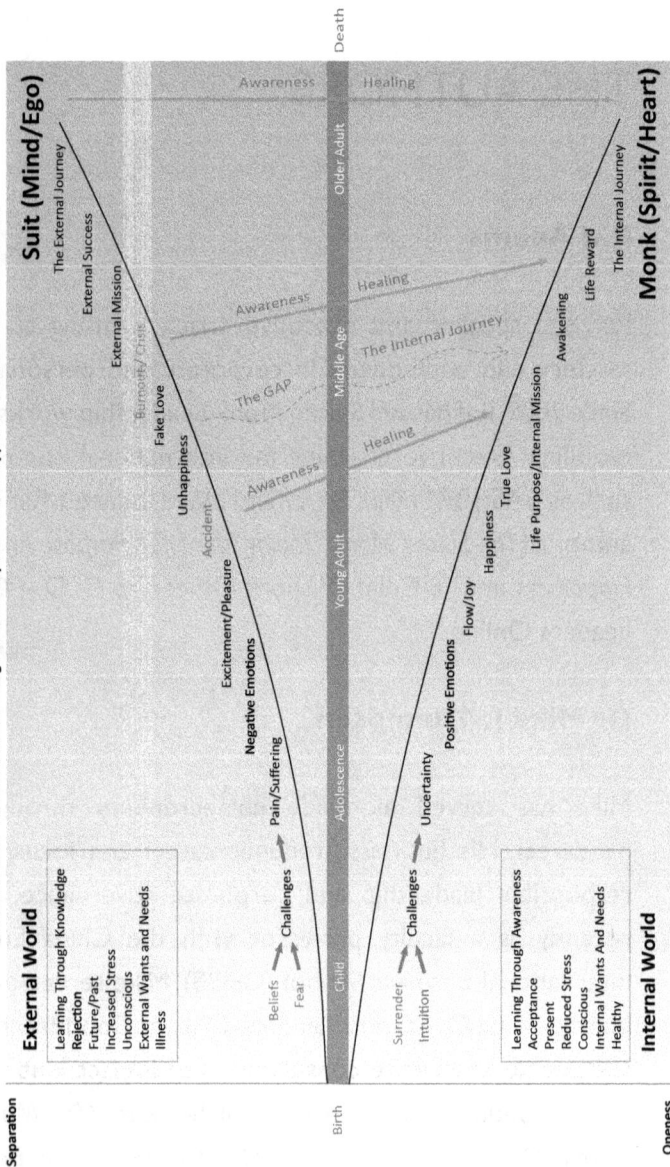

Suit (Mind/Ego)

Monk (Spirit/Heart)

Separation

Oneness

Death

Birth

Awareness   Healing

The External Journey

The Internal Journey

External Success

External Mission

Burnout/Crisis

Fake Love

Unhappiness

Accident

Excitement/Pleasure

Negative Emotions

Pain/Suffering

Challenges

Beliefs

Fear

Older Adult

Middle Age

Young Adult

Adolescence

Child

Awareness   Healing

The Internal Journey

The GAP

Awareness   Healing

Life Reward

Awakening

Life Purpose/Internal Mission

True Love

Happiness

Flow/Joy

Positive Emotions

Uncertainty

Challenges

Surrender

Intuition

External World

Learning Through Knowledge
Rejection
Future/Past
Increased Stress
Unconscious
External Wants and Needs
Illness

Internal World

Learning Through Awareness
Acceptance
Present
Reduced Stress
Conscious
Internal Wants And Needs
Healthy

www.ingramcontent.com/pod-product-compliance
Lightning Source LLC
Chambersburg PA
CBHW071653200326
41519CB00012BA/2504